LOST
LAKE ERIE

LOST
LAKE ERIE

JENNIFER BORESZ ENGELKING

THE
History
PRESS

Published by The History Press
Charleston, SC
www.historypress.com

Front cover: City of Erie, 1900. *Library of Congress*. *Back cover*: Lake Erie sunset. *Photo by author*. *Back cover insert*: The Cyclone roller coaster, Crystal Beach (Ontario), 1930s. *Author's collection*.

First published 2023

Manufactured in the United States

ISBN 9781467153737

Library of Congress Control Number: 2023938437

Notice: The information in this book is true and complete to the best of our knowledge. It is offered without guarantee on the part of the author or The History Press. The author and The History Press disclaim all liability in connection with the use of this book.

To my mom and dad, Mary Joanne and Dale Boresz.

*Thank you for reading to me, encouraging me to write
and going to the beach with me
(where you always let me find the best pieces of beach glass).*

Your love and support mean so much to me.

I love you!

CONTENTS

"Queen of the Lakes"

Queen of the Lakes! Thy throne is fixed where Lake and River meet;
Where trade and commerce proudly lay their treasures at your feet;
Where grand and giant forces move industrial treasures so
That workers see with gratitude trade's still increasing flow.
And Erie, smiling peacefully, or frowning, as she may,
Brings here the commerce of the West from harbors far away!
In majesty the Lake Queen now sits proudly on her throne
And wields a scepter, loyally, on forces all her own!

Songs and Romances of Buffalo, *by John Charles Shea, 1900*

PREFACE

The lure of Lake Erie—if you're reading this book, you likely understand it. Its vastness and beauty draw you in. Its soothing waves calm your soul. It's mesmerizing, like flames in a bonfire, and as intriguing as the promise of lost gold. While gold likely does lie under its surface from the many ships that have lost their battles against the lake's fury, it's the stories woven deep within the waves and along its shoreline that capture our hearts and imaginations.

For those of us, like myself, who live near Lake Erie or once did, it's not just a landmark, but rather a part of who we are. I grew up in Lake County, Ohio, graduated from Cleveland State University and worked as a reporter at CBS stations in Erie, Pennsylvania, and Toledo, Ohio, which allowed me to experience the lake from different vantage points.

My love for Lake Erie began as a child, when I happily visited the beach with my parents and brother, and it has continued into adulthood (along with searching for beach glass, rocks and fossils). Now, I often enjoy heading to Lake Erie's shores with three generations: my parents, my husband and our three children, all of whom appreciate it as much as I do. Through the eyes of my daughter, it's a relaxing "flowing lake of fresh water."

In fact, several of the stories I heard about while growing up near the lake, like the *G.P. Griffith* shipwreck and Willoughbeach Amusement Park in Willowick, inspired me to write my first book, *Hidden History of Lake County, Ohio*. I found so many fascinating stories about Lake County that I decided to write a second book focusing on the lost industry and businesses, called

Lost Lake County, Ohio. As I researched these books, little-known stories of Lake Erie kept popping up, tying into the regions I have worked and lived in.

They are stories of communities and industries that grew in and around the lake, relying on it for fresh drinking water, recreation, industrial resources and the transport of goods. I realized how intertwined they became in the telling of tales, as well as how interconnected we all are. Even though an invisible divide runs down the middle of the lake, separating America and Canada, its waters bring us together, sharing a resource more precious than gold.

The stories in this book relate a variety of these tales, from many different locations, large and small, along and in the lake. It was tough to choose which stories to include, and the ones that made it in did so because they stood out to me. This book is by no means a complete history of Lake Erie. Many wonderful books already exist on that topic (some of which you can find in this book's bibliography). This is a compilation of some of the most intriguing stories that helped make Lake Erie and the region around it what it is today—the good, the bad and the legendary.

I am so thankful for the opportunity to write this book so that I can share these stories with you, and I hope you enjoy reading it as much as I enjoyed writing it!

ACKNOWLEDGEMENTS

I would like to thank John Rodrigue, my commissioning editor at The History Press, for being such a pleasure to work with on my first three books (including this one), along with Senior Editor Ryan Finn and everyone else at The History Press who helped me throughout the publication process.

I'm thankful for so many people in the communities surrounding Lake Erie, at libraries and at historical societies who have helped me track down photos and information for this book, particularly Buffalo & Erie County Public Library, Buffalo, New York; Cleveland Public Library Digital Library; Fairport Harbor Marine Museum and Lighthouse; Hagen History Center, Erie, Pennsylvania; Sandusky Library; HistoricDetroit.org; International Women's Air & Space Museum, Cleveland, Ohio; Library of Congress; Niagara Falls (Ontario) Public Library; the Willoughby-Eastlake Public Libraries; and libraries throughout Northeast Ohio that transferred the many books I used in my research.

Thank you to everyone who has contributed information and/or photos to my book, as noted in the following pages.

Thank you to Andrew McManus, talented artist and architect and husband of my longtime childhood friend Catherine, for creating such a beautiful map of Lake Erie as a reference for the front of my book.

Thank you to the many stores and small businesses that sell my books. Your support is incredible!

Thank you to my amazing friends and, most of all, my wonderful family, especially my parents, Mary Joanne and Dale Boresz, who taught me to chase my dreams, including becoming an author; they have always been my biggest fans, since the earliest days when my stories were written in sloppy handwriting on notebook paper. Thank you to Mary Ann and Dave Engelking, who raised an amazing son who, in turn, became a fantastic husband and father. Thank you for your support!

A big thank-you to my handsome husband, Brian, and our three darling children, who visit me in my "office" (often the couch or kitchen table) with curious questions about what I am writing; they help me make important book decisions and give me quiet time to write when I need it. Thank you for always being as excited as I am about what I am working on and for your constant love. I am so proud of you and blessed to be your Mommy. It is my favorite thing to be and most important role I could ever have. I love you a million times infinity ("more than the sky is high and the ocean is deep and more than there are waves in the ocean and stars in the sky"*).

I'm thankful to God for my family and to have this opportunity to do what I love—research, write and share stories about a region that has always fascinated me and always been my home

Author note: This quote is from *Owly* by Mike Thaler, which was one of my favorite childhood books, read to me over and over again by my mom and dad and later shared with my own children.

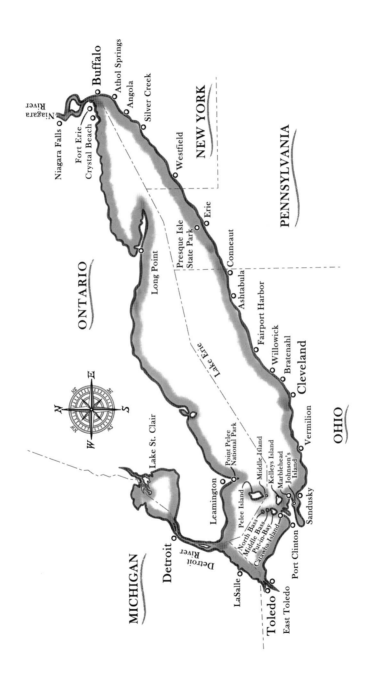

Map of Lake Erie. *Designed by Andrew McManus.*

THE EARLY DAYS

Lake Erie has played a pivotal role in history. As immigrants settled along its shores, major cities developed that became epicenters for industry, including Detroit, Michigan; Toledo and Cleveland, Ohio; Erie, Pennsylvania; and Buffalo, New York, along with hundreds of smaller communities in between.

To understand why so many have been drawn to Lake Erie's shores, let's start with its geology. Its basin was carved out thousands of years ago by glaciers and rivers. Several layers of beach ridges, found miles away from the present shoreline, were left behind from larger versions of the lake that existed before our modern lake, many of which became routes followed by animals and pioneers and are now often roads. Because of this, the lake and its shoreline are a major source of minerals, including sandstone, salt, sand, gypsum, limestone and natural gas.

Lake Erie is the southernmost of the five North American Great Lakes, bordered by the Canadian province of Ontario to the north, the state of New York to the east, Pennsylvania and Ohio to the south and Michigan to the west. It's the fourth largest by surface area and smallest by volume. It's also the shallowest, with an average depth of just sixty-two feet, which means its waters can change quickly depending on the weather, reacting like Jell-O in a giant bowl—a comparison made by my youngest son, "when you touch it, it makes waves in it."

Many a sailor has been caught off guard on the open waters of Lake Erie when the wind whips up, creating powerful waves up to thirteen feet high,

Lake Erie at sunset. *Photo by author.*

tossing them around like toy boats in a bathtub. Due to these treacherous waters, about two thousand shipwrecks are scattered along the lake's floor, and only about four hundred have been discovered, making it among the highest concentration of shipwrecks in the world.

The lake is mainly fed by the Detroit River from Lake St. Clair and drains into the Niagara River and Niagara Falls into Lake Ontario. It may be small, but it is a powerful gatekeeper, connecting the ocean with the upper Great Lakes, allowing immigrants and commerce to cross and spread westward to grow our nation. Like hot lava, it all boils from the lake, spreading knowledge and power outward.

It has been an important shipping route, recreational destination, catalyst for business and industry and an important source of fresh water for millions of pcoplc.

FIRST INHABITANTS

Native Americans, and later pioneers, were drawn to its shorelines, like the Erie Indians, for whom the lake is named, an Iroquoian group that lived in clusters of large longhouses, surrounded by palisade walls, according to Jeff Sherry of the Hagan History Center.

They lived in northern Ohio, parts of northwestern Pennsylvania and western New York and were known by the French in Canada as the "Cat Nation," likely referencing raccoons, panthers or the large number of wildcats in the region.

The Eries were often at war with other Native American tribes, mainly over the fur trade, and were believed to be conquered by the powerful Iroquois Confederacy during the Beaver Wars in 1655. (Since the Iroquois were in what is now the state of New York, they had the advantage of trading with European settlers along the East Coast and acquired more powerful weapons.)

The Iroquois continued to use the land around Lake Erie as hunting grounds until about 1700, when their power waned. Around the same time, other Native American tribes moved into the land, including the Mingo, Ojibwe, Ottawa and Wyandot tribes.

In the 1600s, Lake Erie was the last of the Great Lakes to be discovered by French explorers, who followed rivers and waterways down from the northwest, since the Iroquois, who occupied the Niagara River, were in conflict with the French and didn't allow explorers to pass through.

The land near Lake Erie has also been the site of many Native American battles, including the Battle of Fallen Timbers, which took place on the Maumee River, near present-day Toledo, in 1794. It was a battle over land between the American people pushing to expand westward in the old Northwest Territory and the Native Americans. It resulted in the Indians ceding much of present-day Ohio, which became a state several years later.

WAYNE'S DEFEAT OF THE INDIANS.

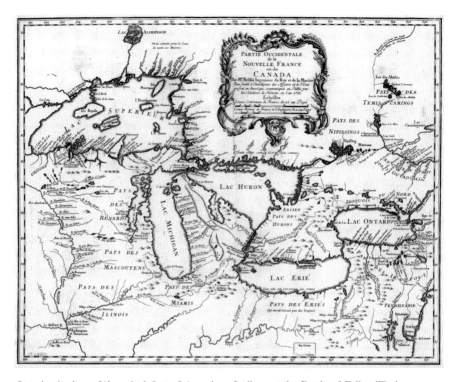

Opposite: Anthony Wayne's defeat of American Indians at the Battle of Fallen Timbers. *Library of Congress.*

Above: French map showing the Great Lakes, 1755. *Library of Congress.*

As pioneers expanded westward in the early nineteenth century, Lake Erie remained a crucial gateway to the new territory and become a critical epicenter for the War of 1812.

BATTLE OF LAKE ERIE

The phrase "Don't give up the ship" has been a rallying cry for centuries. These words can be seen on coffee mugs and T-shirts, particularly in Erie, Pennsylvania, known as "Flagship City" since it was the home port of Commodore Oliver Hazard Perry's flagship, *Niagara*.

During the War of 1812, which began when the United States declared war on Britain, U.S. Navy Captain James Lawrence uttered these now

Commodore Oliver Hazard
Perry, 1917. *Library of Congress.*

famous last words to his crew when he was fatally shot by the British: "Don't give up the ship!"

Shortly after, when his friend and fellow naval officer Commodore Perry arrived in Erie, he renamed the USS *Chesapeake* the USS *Lawrence* after him, according to the website flagdom.com. He also wanted to create a battle flag to encourage his fleet, using Lawrence's last words, so he hired Margaret Foster Steuart, an Erie seamstress, to make it.

"Tensions had been brewing for some time," wrote Jeff Sherry on ErieHistory.org. "Westward expansion of the fast-growing nation was stalled by native tribes of the Midwest and stirred by the British in Canada and by the impressment, basically kidnapping of American sailors on the high seas, all of which fanned the flames."

In August 1812, Fort Detroit, Mackinac and Fort Dearborn, in Chicago, all fell, resulting in British control of the Michigan Territory. Erie ship captain Daniel Dobbins was in Detroit when it fell and made his way back to Erie, where he convinced officials of the need to build a naval squadron on Lake Erie. According to Sherry, he knew just the place to do it: Erie.

"Wood was certainly plentiful around the lakes…but skilled workers, sails, rigging, chains, nails, anchors, metal fittings, paint, guns, ammunition,

Aerial view of Presque Isle Bay in Erie, Pennsylvania, circa 1950s. *Hagen History Center.*

and all the other necessary items were not," wrote Walter Topp on MilitaryHistoryNow.com.

A hastily constructed shipyard was built at the foot of today's Cascade Street, where Dobbins built six ships, including the large brigs *Lawrence* and *Niagara*, with the natural bay formed by Presque Isle peninsula protecting them from Lake Erie's harsh conditions.

"The town of Erie could not even provide housing for the workers who were arriving to build the vessels. In fact, the influx of laborers led to food rationing," wrote Topp. "Even the wood was problematic. The brigs were to be fashioned from trees that had been growing in the forest just a few weeks before. Planks from green or unseasoned wood was [*sic*] prone to warping or splitting once the ships were launched."

But they couldn't wait a year for the wood to dry. The fleet wasn't being constructed to last decades but rather just long enough to win one pivotal battle.

Commodore Perry arrived in Erie that March and, as his fleet was being completed, drilled his crew in ship handling and gunnery skills.

"Meanwhile, the British fleet out of Amherstburg, Ontario, at the western end of the lake, was also making ready for battle," wrote Sherry. "Its commander, Robert Barclay, had similar problems to those of Perry. Short of men and supplies, Barclay sailed his nine ships to Long Point and established it as his headquarters. Barclay effectively blockaded Perry's squadron inside Presque Isle Bay and should have attacked but instead withdrew toward the western end of the lake on July 31, 1813."

Days later, Perry's fleet sailed out into the lake, but the *Niagara* and *Lawrence* were too big to cross the sandbar at the mouth of the bay, so "camels," large wooden barges filled with water, were attached to the brigs' sides. "When pumped out, the ships were lifted high enough to pass over the sandbar refitted with the rigging and other weight that had made passage impossible," noted Sherry. "Perry's fleet set sail for the western end of Lake Erie in search of Barclay."

At dawn on September 10, in Lake Erie near Put-in-Bay, Ohio, Perry readied his men for battle, which didn't include Dobbins because he was sent back to Erie for supplies (he later said that missing the battle was one of his greatest regrets).

As Perry approached six British warships, he was determined to end the naval campaign on Lake Erie that day. "The nine-ship fleet he commanded had been built for this exact moment, and this moment only. If he lost the coming battle his ships would be destroyed, the British would control the lake, and America's Northwest Territory would likely be lost. There would be no opportunity to try again," wrote Topp.

Early in the battle, the British took a heavy toll on the American ships, mainly because their cannons were more accurate at long distances. When the British attacked the *Lawrence*, at least 75 percent of its crew were killed, and it was so badly damaged that Perry transferred ships, along with his

Commodore Oliver Hazard Perry being transferred from the U.S. brig *Lawrence* to the U.S. brig *Niagara. Library of Congress.*

flag, by taking a small longboat to the nearby *Niagara*. Once on board, Perry guided the *Niagara* into battle.

"Before Perry's arrival on the *Niagara*, the ship had hardly engaged the British fleet," according to OhioHistoryCentral.org. "Now, the Niagara and Perry inflicted heavy cannon fire on the British ships. The commander of every British ship was killed or wounded, leaving the British ships under the command of junior officers with limited experience. Perry took advantage of this situation. The *Niagara* rammed the British lead ship while the sailors fired rifles at the British seamen."

"With Captain Barclay mortally wounded aboard his flagship *Detroit*, the British ship began to 'strike their colors,' meaning lowering their flags, as sign of surrender," wrote Sherry. "Perry had won the Battle of Lake Erie. Oliver Hazard Perry would be hailed as a national hero, and the United States, like Perry, was lucky in the remaining War of 1812." It was the first time in U.S. naval history that an entire enemy fleet had been captured. Following his victory, twenty-seven-year-old Perry famously wrote, "We have met the enemy and they are ours. Two ships, two brigs, one schooner and one sloop."

After the battle, Perry and his men returned to Presque Isle Bay to repair their fleet and seek medical treatment for their wounded, according to the Pennsylvania Department of Conservation and Natural Resources. The

Niagara served as a navy receiving ship until it was sunk for preservation, near the *Lawrence*, in Misery Bay in 1820, a circular inlet near the end of Presque Isle peninsula. Nearly a century later, in 1912, the *Niagara* was raised and rebuilt for the one hundredth anniversary of the Battle of Lake Erie in 1913.

"Those enlisted men who were killed in the battle were stitched up into their hammocks, with a cannonball placed at their feet, and their bodies committed to the deep to await the resurrection, when the sea shall give up her dead," wrote William G. Krejci in *Lost Put-in-Bay*. "Tradition held that officers were to be buried on land. Commodore Perry stuck to this tradition. Three American and three British officers were killed in that engagement. Rather than burying them in separate respective burial sites, Perry chose to inter these men together, in one mass grave as equals."

As noted in *Sketches and Stories of the Lake Erie Islands*, written by Lydia Jane Ryall in 1913, nearly half a century after the battle, many of the survivors returned to Put-in-Bay to visit the grave on the island, marked by a tree known as the "Perry willow." "The willow, according to local tradition, grew from a shoot imbedded in the mound by a survivor a few days after the battle," notes Ryall's book. "It took root in the fertile soil and became a stately tree, serving as the only marked place upon the graves."

38. REBUILT "NIAGARA" COMMODORE PERRY'S FLAGSHIP, ERIE, PA.

Rebuilt *Niagara*, 1923. *Author's collection.*

The tree was observed and photographed by thousands until it began showing signs of decay and "fell to earth when scarce a breath of air was stirring" in 1900; islanders allegedly sawed away bits of the tree as souvenirs.

Perry's victory is commemorated at Perry's Victory and International Peace Memorial on Put-in-Bay. His sword and telescope, used in the battle, are on display at the Hagen History Center in Erie, and a reconstructed *Niagara* sits at the Erie Maritime Museum, in the harbor where the original was once constructed.

Author's note: As a reporter for WSEE-TV in Erie in the mid-2000s, I once sailed aboard *Niagara* for a day sail as a feature news story. It was an incredible experience and one of my favorite stories I've had the privilege of covering. It made history come to life!

JOHNSON'S ISLAND

Half a century later, Lake Erie was again playing a central role in a war, this time the Civil War.

The Lincoln administration realized that the Union needed more capacity to house prisoners of war and that northern Ohio, far from the frontlines, was an ideal location. "In October 1861, Lieutenant-Colonel William Hoffman, the Union's commissary-general for prisoners, was ordered to build a new prison among the Lake Erie islands...and to complete the project as quickly as possible," according to Chad Fraser in *Lake Erie Stories*.

Hoffman quickly sailed the islands aboard the *Island Queen*, looking for an appropriate site. North Bass and Middle Bass Islands were too close to Canada, which could make an escape to the neutral British colony too tempting for prisoners. South Bass and Kelleys Islands were home to an emerging winemaking industry, which made the land expensive and would put soldiers close to alcohol.

He found an ideal location closer to the shoreline: Johnson's Island, a small piece of land nestled in between Sandusky and Marblehead Peninsula that could easily be defended and resupplied. With no commercial value, except timber, it could be cheaply leased for $500 per year.

By February, the prison was completed, and the first prisoners arrived in April. At first, it was intended to hold captives of all ranks, but it was later designated for officers only.

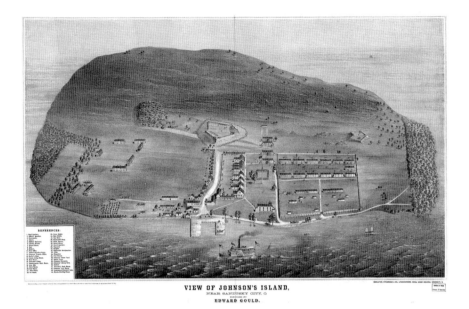

VIEW OF JOHNSON'S ISLAND,
NEAR SANDUSKY CITY, O.
SKETCHED BY
EDWARD GOULD.

View of Johnson's Island near Sandusky, Ohio, a Union prison for Confederate soldiers, 1865. *Library of Congress.*

Hoffman staffed the prison with more than one hundred local men, who received the same pay as soldiers in the field but had the advantage of working close to home.

According to Ryall's *Sketches and Stories of the Lake Erie Islands*, "To further strengthen the island, forts were built. These were furnished each with mounted cannon; while the U.S. gunboat 'Michigan' lay abreast of the prison grounds, her big guns pointing menacingly shoreward."

There was also said to be a detachment of federal troops guarding Johnson's Island, known as the "Gray Beard Brigade" because most of the men were elderly, some allegedly older than eighty.

The prison amenities were better than most, including a library, laundry and two tailors. But the thin-walled barracks made conditions downright life-threatening in the winter, with the bitter winds coming off the lake.

"The two great problems confronting prisoners of war, it has been said, are first, 'How to kill time,' [and] second, 'How to make their escape,'" wrote Ryall. Many prisoners used island resources to save them from boredom, whittling wood or carving buttons and brooches from shells. Other prisoners focused solely on how to get out. One success escape story happened on a brutally cold January night in 1864, when five prisoners used a ladder to climb the fence while guards were napping.

Confederate conspirator John Yates Beall, circa 1861–65. *Library of Congress.*

"Of the five who went over the fence that frigid night, one, who lacked proper clothing, chose to stay behind," wrote Fraser. "The rest made their way across the frozen bay and eventually to Detroit. From there, another death-defying scramble across the partially frozen Detroit River brought them to Canada and safety."

One night in September, men from a Confederate spy ring in Canada hijacked passenger steamship *Philo Parsons*, whose normal route went between Kelleys Island and Sandusky. They wanted to break out the prison's 2,500 Confederate soldiers.

"With John Yates Beall, a former privateer and devoted partisan of the Confederate cause leading them, the hijackers were steaming to the rescue of this unfortunate lot," noted Fraser. "But this would be no easy prison break; first they had to overcome the formidable might of the fourteen-gun USS *Michigan*, the Union warship that guarded the island prison."

When the *Michigan* was nearly in sight, the *Parson* hijackers realized that they didn't have enough wood to power the boat's boiler, so they returned to Middle Bass for more.

Island Queen, headed to Toledo, with a scheduled stop on Middle Bass, pulled in alongside *Parsons*. The *Island Queen* was carrying one hundred passengers, including Union soldiers returning to Toledo, and the increased dock activity made it difficult for Beall's men to hold their cover.

"There was no choice—Beall would have to seize the *Island Queen* or risk being overrun by the soldiers aboard her. Unfortunately, the taking of the *Island Queen* was not done without some bloodshed," wrote Fraser.

Beall knew that he had to get the *Parsons* away from the dock quickly, so he ordered all passengers of both the *Parsons* and *Island Queen* to get off the boats and not tell anyone about what happened for twenty-four hours. The passengers didn't abide by this unofficial maritime agreement and set off in rowboats to tell Put-in-Bay residents about these Confederate raiders.

The hijackers towed the *Island Queen* close to Pelee Island, where they cut the steamer's water feed pipe and set it adrift. They headed back to

Confederate cemetery on Johnson's Island, image taken in 2000. *Library of Congress.*

the *Michigan*, watching for lanterns to flicker as a signal from his men to approach and overtake the ship. However, that signal never came—when word got out from the passengers, the hijacking was called off.

Beall and his men retreated, but in December, the law caught up to him and he was arrested in Dunkirk, New York, while trying to sabotage freight train tracks headed to Buffalo. Beall was found guilty of treason and sentenced to death.

When the war ended soon after, Johnson's Island prison was closed. Prisoners were transferred out, items and fixtures were auctioned off and the walls were torn down. During the forty months the prison existed, about 10,000 men were processed into the stockade, according to JohnsonsIsland.org, peaking in 1864 when the prison held 3,224 prisoners.

After the prison was removed, little happened on the island until 1894, when a small resort was built; it only lasted three years. Another attempt was made in 1904, but it couldn't compete with Cedar Point, across the Sandusky Bay. Cedar Point's owners eventually bought the island and relocated buildings to their resort. Today, the only evidence of the island's Civil War prison are the graves that remain.

STEAMSHIPS

WALK-IN-THE-WATER

On an August afternoon in 1818, *Walk-in-the-Water* arrived in Detroit from Buffalo on its inaugural voyage. It was the first steamship to sail on Lake Erie, and its arrival signaled the beginning of the age of steamship travel on the upper Great Lakes.

It was built in the town of Black Rock, near Buffalo, which was more commercially active than Buffalo at the time, noted Joel Stone in *Floating Palaces of the Great Lakes: A History of Passenger Steamships on the Inland Seas*. "*Walk-in-the-Water*'s hull was fabricated in a newly built shipyard in the wilderness....An abundance of white oak, ash, maple, spruce, and white and red pine grew along the shores of the Scajaquada Creek." The 338-ton steamship was 135 feet long and about 35 feet wide and had the profile of a schooner-rigged barge.

According to *Ohio Lighthouses* by Wil and Pat O'Connel, it transported passengers between Buffalo and Detroit weekly, stopping at Kelleys Island, then known as Cunningham's Island (named for its first European settler), for firewood. "While looked upon with wonder akin to superstitious awe by the now pacified Indians still lingering in the lake regions, the 'Walk-in-the-Water,' was regarded by white settlers of island and mainland, as a marvel of inventive genius, and as a most important adjunct to commercial interests of the lake," wrote Lydia Jane Ryall in *Sketches and Stories of the Lake Erie Islands*.

Walk-in-the-Water, circa 1910–20. *Library of Congress.*

It was named for a Wyandot chief and built to be reliable and profitable, which it was for about three years. "On Oct. 31, 1821, *Walk-in-the-Water* departed Black Rock with a full cargo and good number of passengers," noted Stone. "Captain Rodgers took the vessel into Lake Erie in a light rain but did not anticipate anything adverse. All was well until about eight in the evening."

It was struck by a severe squall, and the shallow lake became rough in moments. "To proceed west was impossible, but attempting to make the river and Black Rock was inherently risky. Captain Rodgers ordered three anchors dropped, one with a chain and two on rope cables. For a long while, the ship and its passengers and crew were at the mercy of the seas. The hull began to leak as the timbers twisted, creating a cacophony of creaks and groans to compete with the gale outside."

At dawn, Rodgers could see that he was close to the beach, just a few hundred yards from the Buffalo Lighthouse, which was then only three years old. "With no options, the captain ordered the anchor chain released and the cables cut with axes. Within a half hour, the hull hit the beach broadside.

Mrs. Thomas Palmer, traveling with her husband and sister-in-law, declared that the first touch was a grazing pass, 'the next swell let her down with a crash of crockery and of glass, [and] the third left her farther up the shore, fixed immovably in the sand. The swells made a clean breach over her. Some of the ladies were in their night clothes, and all were repeatedly drenched,'" notes *Floating Palaces of the Great Lakes*.

Eventually, all passengers and crew were brought ashore, where a lighthouse keeper who saw them floundering was waiting for their arrival. Mrs. Palmer recalled, "[I]t seems to me that I almost flew along the beach, my exhilaration was so great and ran to the lighthouse, where aware of the steamer's plight, a large fire was burning 'in his huge fireplace, by which we remained until carriages came down for us from Buffalo.'"

The townspeople generously made accommodations for the passengers at Landen House, the town's main hotel. The ship had a full cargo, which resulted in a $10,000 to $12,000 loss to its owners. The news of the *Walk-in-the-Water*'s demise led to improvements in lighthouse efficiency and lifesaving capabilities. It was the start of an industry that would affect passenger vessels on the Great Lakes and the development of the region in and around it.

"Steamboating was a way of life for both passengers and crews, involved hundreds of the sleekest and fastest ships in the country, and took guests to nearly every picturesque port around the lakes," Stone wrote. "For a period in the middle of the nineteenth century, the ships elicited the moniker 'palace steamers.' Cabin class guests generally traveled in the elegance and style typically reserved for the very wealthy. Throughout the age, the steamship companies catered to passengers of every type, from immigrants to tourists."

THE GRANDEST STEAMBOAT RACE IN HISTORY: *TASHMOO* VERSUS *CITY OF ERIE*

The wind was whipping off jagged edges of ice, recently broken up on the Detroit River, making way for the latest and greatest steamboat to prepare to launch.

On December 30, 1899, the sidewheel steamship SS *Tashmoo* was cheered on by five hundred spectators who nearly froze as it left the Wyandotte yards of the Detroit Shipbuilding Company. It was the same site where it was built along with 133 vessels, large and small, that launched before it. "Never was a boat launched under the same conditions as the *Tashmoo* and never was a

Tashmoo leaving Detroit wharf, 1901. *Library of Congress.*

boat more successfully dropped into its element," reads the December 31, 1899 *Detroit Free Press*.

The *Tashmoo* was designed by Frank E. Kirby, who designed Detroit's Boblo boats—the *Columbia* and the *Ste. Claire* (which brought passengers to and from Boblo Island Amusement Park for nearly a century)—along with several stately night boats, including *City of Detroit III*. According to Dan Austin on HistoricDetroit.org, many consider Kirby the greatest Great Lakes architect of all time and the father of modern ice-breaking technology.

The *Tashmoo* was a day boat that could accommodate four thousand passengers and had elegant parlors taking the place of state rooms on overnight steamboats. "She will be fitted up magnificently. Her main deck will have an elegant cabin, the front portion of which will be a grand saloon, fitted out in quartered oak," according to the *Free Press* article. A grand staircase led to the saloon above, and a large dining room could seat several hundred people at once.

By June, it was ferrying passengers on excursions through the waterways of Detroit, stopping between Port Huron, Detroit and Tashmoo Park, developed by the White Star Line, which also owned the *Tashmoo* several years earlier.

The White Star Line bought sixty acres on Harsens Island in northern Lake St. Clair, which it developed as a resort destination with a bathhouse, dance pavilion, picnic areas, ball diamond and eventually rides. The *Tashmoo*, nicknamed the "White Flyer" and the "Glass Hack" for its many windows, was built to carry passengers to the newly developed Tashmoo Park.

At the time, it was considered the fastest ship on the Great Lakes, and the owner was so convinced of its speed that he made a $1,000 bet to any boat that could beat it. SS *City of Erie* accepted the challenge. It was built in 1898 by the Detroit Dry Dock Company, in Cleveland, for the Cleveland Buffalo Transit Company.

According to a Cleveland.com article by Laura Johnston, the *City of Erie* carried passengers between Cleveland, Erie and Buffalo, earning the nickname the "Honeymoon Special" because many couples aboard were celebrating their marriages.

The *Tashmoo* was 329 feet long and 70 feet wide, with a slim nose built for speed, while the *City of Erie* was 324 feet long and 78 feet wide. The

City of Erie at Buffalo, New York. *Library of Congress.*

City of Erie, 1900. *Library of Congress.*

Tashmoo was favored to win and even had a correspondent from the *Detroit Free Press* riding aboard during the infamous race on June 4, 1901, when the two sidewheel steamships would race from Cleveland to Erie to determine the fastest ship on the Great Lakes.

According to the *Detroit Free Press* correspondent the day after the race, thousands of people lined the shores from Cleveland to Erie, and thousands more were on the water, waiting for a glimpse of the race. Thousands of dollars were bet on the outcome. "For four hours and nineteen minutes she [*City of Erie*] struggled with Detroit's splendid steamship *Tashmoo*, and when it was all over and the two magnificent craft had raced for nearly a hundred miles, they were but a few boat lengths apart," wrote the unnamed correspondent.

The *Tashmoo* had more horsepower, with 2,500 IHP versus *City of Erie*'s 2,200, and drew in less water. However, what amounted to less than a minute of time determined the race's winner. "In the grandest steamboat race in the history of American navigation, the Buffalo steamer *City of Erie*, today established her right to the title 'Queen of the Inland Seas,'" reads the *Detroit Free Press*'s June 4, 1901 article.

According to Dan Austin on HistoricDetroit.org, *City of Erie* had come prepared, which may have helped it win, with deck chairs removed to cut back on wind resistance, along with all unnecessary items to lighten its weight. "Others said that the *Tashmoo* repeatedly went off course," wrote Austin. "Some said that the *Tashmoo* had condenser problems on its engine, while the *City of Erie*'s condenser was packed in ice to keep it from overheating."

Only the crew on each steamboat really know what happened that day, but the outcome is undisputed: *City of Erie* crossed the finish line a mere forty-five seconds before *Tashmoo*.

After the Race

CITY OF ERIE

Nearly a decade after the race, *City of Erie* met its dramatic end. A September 28, 1909 *New York Times* article reads, "On Lake Erie, off Dunkirk, early today [September 27] the schooner *T. Vance Straubenstein* ran into the course of the steamer *City of Erie*. The vessels collided and the schooner was sunk."

Two seamen were rescued from the *Straubenstein*, but the captain, mate and female cook drowned. In 1938, the *City of Erie* was retired and later scrapped in Cleveland.

TASHMOO

For several decades, visitors to Tashmoo Park, referred to as the "western Venice" by the *Detroit-News Tribune*, enjoyed the relaxing two-hour ride from Detroit aboard the *Tashmoo*. The steamship even provided rides on the Detroit River to Henry Ford and President Theodore Roosevelt.

An old steamship tradition warned that giving them a Native American name was bad luck. *Tashmoo*, which meant "at the great spring" in Wampanoag, seemed to back up that sentiment. When a nasty winter storm blew through metro Detroit on the night of December 8, 1927, fourteen heavy cables that secured it to the dock snapped, and it drifted upstream, colliding with the Douglas MacArthur Bridge, which led to Belle Isle, suffering minor injuries, according to Austin.

Then, in 1934, high winds struck again and blew *Tashmoo* onto a sandbar near the park. Passengers were unloaded by tugboats and a paddle was damaged, but it was quickly repaired and back in the water.

Opposite, top: *Tashmoo* at Tashmoo Park, St. Clair Flats, Michigan, circa 1900–1920. *Library of Congress.*

Opposite, bottom: President Theodore Roosevelt waving his hat aboard the *Tashmoo*, October 18, 1902. *Library of Congress.*

Above: Detroit skyline, with signs for Tashmoo and Bob-Lo Parks, circa 1910–30. *Library of Congress.*

Two years later, while carrying about 1,400 passengers back to Detroit after an evening of dancing on Sugar Island, it hit a rock and began taking on water. The crew navigated it to a dock in Amherstburg, Ontario, where everyone got off, but *Tashmoo* sank in less than twenty feet of water.

When a salvage crew arrived to lift it from the riverbed, it broke in half. It was pulled by tugs to Boblo Island a month later where its engines were removed and the once great *Tashmoo* was later scrapped.

With the loss of its steamer, Tashmoo Park lost much of its appeal, and business decreased dramatically, closing in 1951. It was later sold and turned into a marina, where some original structures are said to remain.

SS *EASTLAND*

A bell rings out from a clock sitting on a shelf inside the Fairport Harbor Marine Museum and Lighthouse in Lake County, Ohio. It looks like any old maritime clock, once used to mark time aboard a ship, but if you look closely, you'll see the name of the ship from whence it came etched upon its face: *Steamer Eastland*. It suffered the worst fate of any ship on the Great Lakes.

On July 24, 1915, after more than 2,500 passengers boarded to head to a picnic on the shores of Lake Michigan, it rolled over at its Chicago dock, and more than 840 people died. "People were trapped below decks, screaming and unable to climb out," reads *Ohio Lighthouses*. "So horrible were newspaper pictures and accounts of people dying that the mere mention of the name *Eastland* could evoke fear and trembling."

Eastland, owned by the St. Joseph–Chicago Steamship Company at the time, was launched in 1903. According to History.com, it was designed to carry 650 passengers, but major retrofitting in 1913 allowed for the boat to carry up to 2,500 people. That same year, a naval architect told officials that it still had structural defects and, if not fixed, there could be a serious accident.

Although the disaster took place in Chicago, *Eastland* had prior Lake Erie ties. In 1908, Cleveland investors bought it to take passengers from Cleveland to Cedar Point amusement park, which it did for about five years.

An ad from the time reads, "When you visit Cleveland this summer, don't fail to take a ride on the all-steel constructed…safest twin-screw steamer on the Great Lakes: *Steamer Eastland*. Fare $1 for round trip. Five hours at the Point. Won't sink and can't burn."

According to the Sandusky Library Archives Research Center on SanduskyHistory.blogspot.com, a song was even written by S.J. Monk in 1911 called "On the Boat Eastland," considered the waltz hit that summer, which began, "A-hoy! for the breeze off Lake E-rie's smooth seas, and a Steam-er grand….On a fine glass-y floor, far a-way out from shore, on the boat East-land."

Its final Cleveland to Cedar Point route season was 1913, when it carried about 200,000 people, entertaining them with a steam calliope (a musical steam-whistle organ) during their ride.

But that isn't the only Lake Erie connection. Lifelong Fairport Harbor resident and local historian John Ollila welcomed me to the Fairport Harbor Marine Museum and Lighthouse to research this book. He not only shared

Clock from the *Eastland*, donated to the Fairport Harbor Marine Museum and Lighthouse by the family of Captain Merwin Thompson. *Photo by author.*

Eastland after it capsized. *Photo donated to Fairport Harbor Marine Museum and Lighthouse by Captain Thompson's family members.*

Eastland returning from Cedar Point by moonlight. *Author's collection.*

the information about the *Eastland* clock, but he also showed me cabin lights from the ill-fated steamer, on display in the museum. They were donated by the granddaughter of Captain Merwin Stone Thompson, from nearby Painesville, Ohio, who was once the captain of the ship.

I'm thankful that Ollila suggested I read Captain Thompson's memoir, *An Ancient Mariner Recollects*, published in 1966 when he was ninety-one years old, in which he recounts many of his memories associated with the *Eastland*.

Thompson's family had roots in Cleveland and Vermilion, and several relatives were sailors and shipbuilders on Lake Erie. He followed in their footsteps and worked his way up on sailing vessels on the lake. "I was interested in the *Eastland* and secretly I had been wanting an opportunity to handle her, so I was delighted to be appointed master for the year 1909," he wrote in his memoir. "Soon I found there were new problems with which to cope for this excursion business was all new to me."

One was the large number of passengers and their many different personalities. Captain Thompson recalled:

> *I found myself a vantage point from which I could observe the unloading and loading of some 5,000 people, which had to be accomplished in about forty-five minutes to leave for the evening run. I armed myself with an*

The Eastland with a 1909 July 4th cruise crowd of 2,500 on board just before sailing from Cleveland. Capt. M. S. Thompson is standing at the end of the bridge wing.

Captain Merwin Thompson on board the *Eastland*, July 4, 1909, carrying 2,500 passengers from Cleveland. *Photo donated to Fairport Harbor Marine Museum and Lighthouse by Captain Thompson's family members.*

efficient but easily concealed loaded leather billy club. It proved its worth on one memorable occasion. We were unloading the Cedar Point passengers at Cleveland when some stupid person thought it would be a great joke to scream "FIRE." That was once when my billy club did its work and the would-be joker found himself being escorted to our detention room to think it over and recover from the effects of Sandusky beer, for the Eastland *was a dry boat.*

Thompson also described the ship's unique steam calliope, with its pipes and keyboard placed between the smokestacks on the hurricane deck:

The calliope on this boat is the only one I ever heard of, before or since, on stern paddle wheel boats, except in a circus parade. The piano player in our orchestra did a little double duty. He played the calliope for fifteen minutes before leaving time in the morning at Cleveland and on leaving

Cedar Point at 4:30 P.M. He also played for fifteen minutes before leaving on the moonlight trip. When weather conditions were good, our musical instrument could be heard for a distance of a mile or more.

He wrote that Cleveland's sidewheel steamer *Goodtime*, which nearly took the same course to Put-in-Bay, left its dock every morning fifteen minutes before *Eastland*, but *Eastland* was faster and passed the *Goodtime* near Lorain. As the *Eastland* passed, the piano player couldn't resist loudly playing a popular tune from the time, "The Girl I Left Behind Me."

In 1909, the *Eastland* was equipped with wireless communication, which was still in its infancy, so he sent a message to his four-year-old daughter, which was the first wireless message received in Painesville, Ohio, where they lived. (A year earlier, on July 17, 1908, the first ship-to-shore message was sent from the yacht *Thelma*, which was reviewing yacht races between Put-in-Bay and Sandusky.)

Several years after being captain of the *Eastland*, Thompson was stopped by police while driving from Painesville to Cleveland. "The officer and several men seemed highly pleased with themselves in capturing me and even stated how lucky they were to be the successful ones; police had been stationed at all other routes from Painesville to Cleveland with instructions to stop me in any event."

The officers asked if he was the former captain of the *Eastland* and told him that it had capsized at 7:20 a.m. that morning. He wrote, "I think I replied, 'That is hard to believe. It seems impossible; I was master of that ship three years, carried well over twenty-five thousand people during that period without one single claim, personal or otherwise on my company or underwriters. Neither was I ever reprimanded by the United States Steamboat Inspectors.'"

Thompson was called in to testify as an expert witness on the stability of the steamer *Eastland*, and after lengthy court proceedings, the case was dropped and there were no convictions. He believes that the cause of the disaster was a tragic misunderstanding between the bridge officers and engine room department regarding the distribution of water ballast.

After the accident, the *Eastland* was taken to a shipyard and sold to the U.S. government. The navy converted and renamed it the *Wilmette*, using it for naval training on the Great Lakes until 1948, when it was decommissioned and sold to a scrap company. According to Thompson, "Thus writing 'finish' to the story of the *Eastland-Wilmette* who was heralded at one time as the speed queen of the Great Lakes."

SS *AQUARAMA*

Today, travel between Detroit and Cleveland is mainly done by car, but for a few short years in the 1950s and '60s, passengers could climb aboard the SS *Aquarama* to cruise to these cities on Lake Erie.

Tom Miller of Bratenahl, Ohio, remembered when he sailed on the *Aquarama* in 1962. He said the trip was organized by the Shaker Heights Mercer Elementary School summer day camp, and he remembered the things that impressed him the most as a kid, including lots of pinball machines, junk food and a very loud air horn. "Most of the details are hazy. I don't think we got off the ship in Detroit, we just turned around and headed for home. Smooth sailing."

According to Case Western Reserve University's (CWRU) Encyclopedia of Cleveland History, "The *Aquarama*, the largest passenger ship to operate on the Great Lakes, was built in 1945 in Chester, PA as a troop transport ship named the *Marine Star*."

In 1953, the 520-foot ship was bought by Sand Products Company of Detroit and went through a two-year, $8 million conversion to a nine-deck luxury-class ferry renamed *Aquarama*. It debuted at Chicago's Navy Pier, wrote Joel Stone in his book *Floating Palaces of the Great Lakes*, and local papers advertised the "Aquarama Water Thrill Show," as well as dining and dancing.

According to CWRU, "The first new liner on the Great Lakes in 20 years, the ship was capable of carrying 2,500 passengers and 160 cars and featured full picture windows, five bars, soda fountains, four restaurants, two dance floors, a movie theater, a television theater, a children's playroom, and all the latest marine equipment, including a gyro compass, a radio direction finder, radar, a fathometer, and ship-to-shore phones. Its cruising speed was 22 mph."

In 1957, *Aquarama* began transporting passengers between the two cities in about six hours. According to the 1957 SS *Aquarama* Summer Sailing Schedule, it was "an exhilarating delightful new cruising experience across scenic Lake Erie," operating from June 21 through September 15.

Passengers like Ursula Carleton, who grew up in Cleveland's Collinwood neighborhood, could get a round-trip ticket for less than ten dollars. Carleton recalled riding *Aquarama* in June 1961. She had just graduated from Collinwood High School, where she and her friend Cora Sue took a night mechanic class to learn how to change oil and set calibers. (She said that the boys didn't like having girls in the class and told them to "go take cake decorating class," but neither would listen.) Ursula, Cora Sue and two other friends all set sail on *Aquarama* just weeks after two of them graduated.

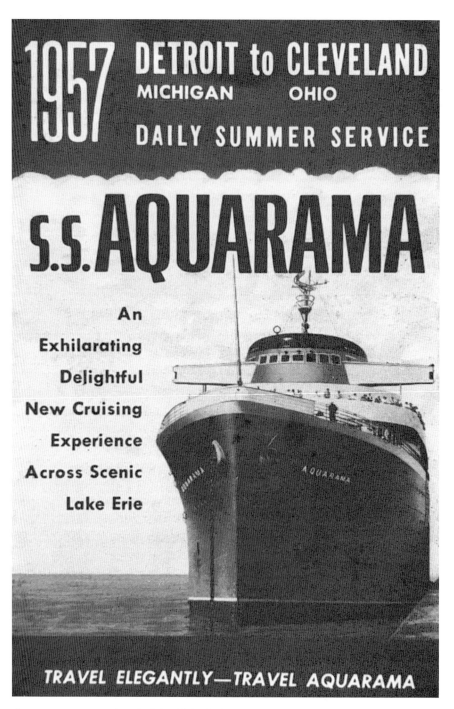

Aquarama summer service schedule, 1957. *Author's collection.*

MICHIGAN-OHIO NAVIGATION COMPANY
1957 S. S. AQUARAMA SUMMER SAILING SCHEDULE
STARTING FRIDAY, JUNE 21ST AND ENDING SUNDAY, SEPTEMBER 15TH

SOUTHBOUND TO CLEVELAND		NORTHBOUND TO DETROIT
Lv. Detroit 12:01 AM EST—Ar. Cleveland 7:00 AM EDST Lv. Detroit 4:00 PM EST—Ar. Cleveland 11:00 PM EDST	**SUN.**	Lv. Cleveland 8:15 AM EDST—Ar. Detroit 1:30 PM EST
Lv. Detroit 4:00 PM EST—Ar. Cleveland 11:00 PM EDST	**MON.**	Lv. Cleveland 8:15 AM EDST—Ar. Detroit 1:30 PM EST
Lv. Detroit 4:00 PM EST—Ar. Cleveland 11:00 PM EDST	**TUES.**	Lv. Cleveland 8:15 AM EDST—Ar. Detroit 1:30 PM EST
Lv. Detroit 8:15 AM EST—Ar. Cleveland 3:15 PM EDST	**WED.**	Lv. Cleveland 12:01 AM EDST—Ar. Detroit 5:15 AM EST Lv. Cleveland 5:45 PM EDST—Ar. Detroit 11:00 PM EST
Lv. Detroit 8:15 AM EST—Ar. Cleveland 3:15 PM EDST	**THUR.**	Lv. Cleveland 5:45 PM EDST—Ar. Detroit 11:00 PM EST
Lv. Detroit 8:15 AM EST—Ar. Cleveland 3:15 PM EDST	**FRI.**	Lv. Cleveland 5:45 PM EDST—Ar. Detroit 11:00 PM EST
Lv. Detroit 8:15 AM EST—Ar. Cleveland 3:15 PM EDST	**SAT.**	Lv. Cleveland 5:45 PM EDST—Ar. Detroit 11:00 PM EST

EST Denotes Eastern Standard Time	EDST Denotes Eastern Daylight Saving Time

BUDGET FARE VOYAGES
WEEK DAY SAILINGS MONDAY THROUGH FRIDAY

CLASS OF TRAFFIC	LOUNGE FARE	CLUB FARE
One Way Passengers (Accompanying Automobiles)	$5.23 (plus tax) *2.62 " "	$7.00 (plus tax) *3.50 " "
One Way Passengers (Trip Passage Only)	5.23 " " *2.62 " "	7.00 " " *3.50 " "
Round Trip Passengers (Seven Day Stop-Over)	9.41 " " *4.71 " "	12.59 " " *6.30 " "
Continuous Cruise Passengers (2½ Hour Stop-Over)	7.73 " " *3.87 " "	10.82 " " *5.41 " "
Group Continuous Cruise Passengers (50 to 150 Advance Ticket Sales)	7.11 " " *3.56 " "	9.96 " " *4.98 " "
Group Continuous Cruise Passengers (Over 150 Advance Ticket Sales)	6.80 " " *3.40 " "	
Tourist Auto Rate—One Way	8.74 " "	8.74 " "

REGULAR FARE VOYAGES
SATURDAY, SUNDAY AND HOLIDAY SAILINGS

CLASS OF TRAFFIC	LOUNGE FARE	CLUB FARE
One Way Passengers (Accompanying Automobiles)	$5.23 (plus tax) *2.62 " "	$7.00 (plus tax) *3.50 " "
One Way Passengers (Trip Passage Only)	5.23 " " *2.62 " "	7.00 " " *3.50 " "
Continuous Cruise Passengers (2½ Hour Stop-Over)	8.64 " " *4.32 " "	11.82 " " *5.91 " "
Group Continuous Cruise Passengers (50 to 150 Advance Ticket Sales)	7.95 " " *3.98 " "	10.87 " " *5.44 " "
Group Continuous Cruise Passengers (Over 150 Advance Ticket Sales)	7.60 " " *3.80 " "	
Tourist Auto Rate—One Way	8.74 " "	8.74 " "
*Children—Age 5 to 11 years inclusive when accompanied by full-fare passenger.		

Aquarama summer service schedule interior, 1957. *Author's collection.*

She said it was their first "ocean voyage" and that they were very impressed with the size of the ship. "It was fun for us. We just strolled around and looked at everything and enjoyed ourselves. We had coffee or pop. We went to Detroit and got off for a little while and went home."

The success of *Aquarama* depended on fast runs and quick turnarounds. According to Stone, it had three runs per day, with each leg taking five hours and twenty minutes, leaving only twenty minutes to offload thousands of people and hundreds of cars and then reload and depart.

The book goes on to say, "*Aquarama*'s deepwater hull design threw a mighty wake, which was blamed for swamping fishing boats and ripping docks from riverside boardwalks." This led to complaints and lawsuits that forced the ship to check its speed in the river.

According to Stone, throughout its career several accidents tarnished its reputation:

> *While finishing its tour and preparing for a run to Cleveland in 1956, the* Aquarama *was unable to turn in the Detroit River and ran straight into the Windsor seawall. The following year, on its inaugural*

run on the Detroit-Cleveland route, it had similar problems. Later that same season, it was blown in the Detroit News' docks. In 1959, while departing the Cleveland wharf, wind caught the ship's nose, and it clipped the stern of the massive USS Macon. In 1962 it grounded entering the harbor at Cleveland, and when the drawbridge did not hoist fast enough, its stern mast snagged on a cable. The cable snapped, and the mast was severely bent.

Although *Aquarama* was popular, it wasn't very profitable, due to its massive size, lack of overnight accommodations and high operating costs. There were complaints of long lines and poor service that forced the company to decrease capacity from 2,500 to 1,800.

Aquarama sailed its last trip in September 1962 and was kept at a Muskegon dock until a Canadian company bought it for $3 million in 1987. It was towed to Windsor, where it stayed on the shoreline until the mid-1990s, when there were plans to turn it into a floating casino and rechristen it *Marine Star*. However, legal obstacles ensued, and a little more than a decade later, it was scrapped.

The ship may be gone, but many still recall their memorable trips aboard *Aquarama*, when miles of asphalt were replaced with wind in their hair and a view of the shoreline as they cruised across the lake.

The age of steamships began with such grandeur, but they gradually faded away as competing modes of transportation like trains and cars took over. In 1967, the steamship reign ended in the Great Lakes when the *North American* made its final voyage from Detroit, with a stop in Cleveland, to Montreal. When the ship arrived, passengers reluctantly disembarked, knowing full well that the Great Lakes era of steamships had come to an end.

TRANSPORTATION

Transportation in, and along, Lake Erie evolved over the years, from stagecoaches, steamships and trains to cars and modern cargo ships. Each mode of transportation has helped bring immigrants and commerce into the Lake Erie region and holds an important place in its history.

ANGOLA HORROR TRAIN WRECK

Big Sister Creek is a peaceful place for fishing or relaxing. It meanders through Angola, New York, to reach Lake Erie a few miles to the west. One spot along the idyllic creek is the site of a tragic train wreck that put the small town on the map on December 18, 1867.

The Buffalo & Erie Railroad's "New York Express" train was traveling from Cleveland to Buffalo (about twenty-two miles northeast of Angola) and was running behind schedule. According to Atlas Obscura, the train was designed to work on different gauge tracks, which could lead to instability.

As it crossed the high truss bridge over Big Sister Creek (now Mill Street Bridge), the last car jumped the track (partly due to a slightly bent front axle) and derailed, causing it to crash into the gorge below. "The accident caused the stoves to overturn, throwing hot coals all over the car and the passengers," reads Atlas Obscura. The cars were made of wood, and the kerosene lamps aboard quickly spread the fire. "The first car fell into the creek gorge and

A portion of a map from *The Illustrated Handbook for Travelers through the United States*, showing railroads, canals and stagecoach roads, 1846. *Library of Congress.*

became an inferno," according to WBFO.org. "A second car also derailed, but all but one person were believed rescued. 19 or 20 of the victims were burned beyond recognition."

Around fifty people died, and one hundred were injured, in the accident that became known as the "Angola Horror." A memorial service was held for the victims at the Exchange Street train depot in Buffalo three days before Christmas, and nineteen wooden boxes, with unidentified remains, were buried at Forest Lawn Cemetery. According to WBFO.org, if you go there today, you'll find an open plot of land. The railroad company said that it was going to put a headstone up but never did.

The accident spurred public outrage, which led to improvements in railway safety, ensuring that stoves would be properly secured in cars and track gauges standardized. It also led to the development of air brakes and banning of wooden cars, according to WBFO.org.

Business magnate and at one time richest person in America John D. Rockefeller of Cleveland had a ticket to be on that train. His luggage even made it aboard. However, he was running late that morning and missed it. He took a train later in the day, and after arriving in Angola, he telegraphed his wife in Cleveland, saying, "Thank God I am unharmed."

You can find a marker memorializing the tragedy off Mill Street where a car bridge now goes over Big Sister Creek. According to Atlas Obscura, if you follow the creek six hundred feet upstream, you can still see the remnants of the train bridge's concrete embankment.

LAKE ERIE ISLAND MAIL SERVICE

In the late 1800s, U.S. Mail service between the Lake Erie islands and mainland was extremely treacherous. The Put-in-Bay mail crossed twice a day, covering miles of ice, according to *Sketches and Stories of the Lake Erie Islands*.

"The individual who fills the position of mail carrier must be possessed of agility and alertness, unflinching courage and physical endurance," reads the book. "He must thoroughly understand the ice, its foibles and weaknesses; must know where the undercurrents, which wear it, are strongest, and be able to locate shoals and sunken reefs—dangerous to the ice navigator as to the mariner."

To do so, this brave postal worker traveled across the lake in a unique boat. "For rapid transit from place to place, the ice yacht is an object of utility, and when conditions are favorable, it is sometimes used in carrying the mails, though the iron sheeted mail boat used for this purpose is fitted with oars, sails, and sled runners. The sails may be used either on ice or on water; so that the craft is practically a combination sailboat, rowboat, ice yacht, and sled."

Sometimes postal workers got out to drag their boat along or forced it through the ice using oars and pike-poles to break up the sheets, and sometimes they even walked across with their mail bags slung over their shoulders.

The book notes that one of the most hazardous experiences was during the winter of 1897, when the Hitchcock brothers were caught in a storm while attempting to deliver mail and became wedged in a drift of snow

Veteran Lake Erie island mail carrier Henry Elfers, circa late 1800s. *From* Sketches and Stories of the Lake Erie Islands.

U.S. Mail service in winter to Kelley's Island, Ohio, circa early 1900s. *Sandusky Library.*

and ice that carried them down the lake. Islanders thronged the shores looking for them. The conditions were so bad that they were assumed dead. Yet somehow they made it ashore. "On arrival at home their friends were obliged to cut and tear from them their ice-armored clothing which they exchanged for warm, dry garments," reads the book.

Henry Elfers, a veteran Kelleys Island mail carrier for more than forty years, had many close calls on the ice. Part of an interview with a newspaper reporter, published in *Sketches and Stories of the Lake Erie Islands*, details his adventures:

> *When I was a youngster I was out in a boat all the time. Now I don't care for ordinary sailing, but battling with the ice has a fascination for me. As soon as ice begins to form I feel eager to get out one of the ironclads and fight my way across.*

His "ironclads" were flat-bottomed skiffs, fourteen feet wide and sixteen feet long, with a sail in the bow to carry the vessel through water or over ice and two iron-shod runners on the bottom to be used as a sled:

From here to Sandusky is ten miles in a direct line and I go there when the conditions are good. At other times I go to Marblehead, which is four miles away, and the nearest point on the mainland. I have sailed those four miles over smooth ice in 20 minutes. I have covered the same distance in eight hours. That was when the ice was about one- and one-half inches thick and I had to break my way over every foot of the four miles. At times the lake has been covered with icebergs, 20 to 30 feet high, and I have had to travel 15 miles in a roundabout course to reach Marblehead. Often, I have to traverse alternating sheets of clear water and fields of ice, and I can tell you it is hard, tedious work.

In the winter of 1896, Elfers and his son were caught in a blizzard while delivering the mail. They were half a mile away from the island, with temperatures below zero, fifty-five-mile-per-hour winds and snow falling so thickly he couldn't see his son on the other end of his boat. "We could not land here on account of rotten ice banked against the shore and had to fight our way back to Marblehead," he explained. "Spray broke over the boat and our clothing was a mass of ice. The sail was torn to pieces. We battled with the blizzard four hours before we succeeded in reaching Marblehead."

THE FIRST CAR TRIP ACROSS LAKE ERIE

On an icy winter day in the late 1800s or early 1900s, a group of five men on Catawba Island decided to pile into a car and drive across the frozen lake.

It started out as a joke among friends, according to Lydia Jane Ryall's *Sketches and Stories of the Lake Erie Islands*, but as the car advanced without sinking, the idea of crossing grew on the group (consisting of J.P. Cangney, John Darr, Captain Wallace Smith, L.B. DeWitt and J.C. West).

First, they drove to Put-in-Bay, crossed to North Bass Island and then on to Pelee Island. They were joined by Dr. O.B. Van Epps, who must have thought that it seemed a safe enough venture to tag along for the remainder of the trip. After leaving Pelee, they headed northward to Leamington.

However, large cracks in the ice kept them from their destination. They were not deterred. To cross, two men stood on either side of the crack to "help" if needed. "Then backing the machine about fifty feet, the driver sent it forward at topmost speed, clearing the crack at a flying leap," Ryall wrote.

As they neared Leamington, they had another hurdle: a ten- to twelve-foot-wide crack that was too big to try to jump over. "After deliberation they

Top: Five men traveling across the ice on Lake Erie in an automobile, circa late 1800s/early 1900s. *From* Sketches and Stories of the Lake Erie Islands.

Bottom: Four men out of the car while traveling across the ice on Lake Erie, circa late 1800s/early 1900s. *From* Sketches and Stories of the Lake Erie Islands.

decided to follow the course of the opening, hoping that it might narrow to a point that would permit of a crossing being made. In this they were disappointed, however; but after following the crack a considerable distance they reached a point at which the water was bridged with sixteen-foot lengths of heavy boards."

As luck would have it, a sled load of tobacco and its driver from Pelee, bound for Leamington, reached the obstructing crack just as a load of lumber got there, and part of the timber was used to build a bridge across the crack. Thanks to the wooden bridge, they made it to Leamington, spent the night and traveled through a heavy snowstorm the next day to make their way back to Catawba Island. It's unknown whether this group of friends ever made a repeat trip.

POPE-TOLEDO AUTOMOBILE

For most, cars were an unattainable novelty in the early 1900s. But for a few, they were a status symbol, putting them at the height of luxury. The Pope-Toledo car, at a base price of nearly $3,000, several times the annual salary of most Americans at the time, was aimed at the rich and elite.

It all started with Colonel Albert Augustus Pope, an ambitious industrialist from Hartford, Connecticut, who dominated the American bicycle industry in the late 1800s and was turning his sights on the auto industry.

In 1900, the American Bicycle Company (ABC), one of Pope's companies, built a steam truck in a factory on Central Avenue in Toledo, Ohio. According to ToledosAttic.org, he began buying patents and properties in the early days of the automotive industry. He built his first prototype of a single-engine car at his shop in Connecticut in 1903. According to the Stahl's Auto Website, production began the following year with two body style options.

By 1904, the International Bicycle Company had begun making Toledo steam cars, which were built and promoted as more efficient, requiring less gasoline. Both steam and electric cars had a limited travel range—electrics needed to be charged every fifty to sixty miles, while steamers needed to replenish their water supply, going through a gallon of water for every mile traveled, which meant that the Toledo Steamers could only travel about thirty-six miles at a time.

Two Toledo Steamer models took part in the country's first long-distance endurance road rally, from New York to Buffalo. Although the race was canceled en route due to the news that President William McKinley had been assassinated, a 6.5-horsepower Toledo earned a third-class certificate after finishing the race at an average of 4.21 miles per hour. According to the website Toledo's Attic, "[P]leased by Toledo's prospects, ABC announced a few months later that it was moving the headquarters of its automobile division from New York to Toledo and expanding its factory by a third."

Above: Pope Motor Car Company, Toledo, Ohio. *Paul Wohlfarth.*

Opposite: Cover of Pope-Toledo brochure. *Paul Wohlfarth.*

ABC changed its name to the International Motor Car Company, and the Toledo plant began building its first internal combustion touring cars, along with a line of steamers.

The newly renamed "Pope-Toledo" was a four-wheel, front-engine two-seater with a wooden chassis (frame). It was a sturdy, ruggedly built open roadster with high, overstuffed seats, according to Toledo's Attic. A second model was a larger touring car able to seat five people.

Paul Wohlfarth bought a Pope-Toledo brochure at an auction in Monroe, Michigan, and generously shared its content with the author. The cover reads, "Home of the Toledo Touring Cars. The Largest Automobile Plant in the World." Inside the brochure, the company describes the value to expect when purchasing a Pope-Toledo:

> [W]*e feel that the world-wide reputation and reliability of "Toledo" cars are a sufficient guarantee to all prospective purchasers that in building, no expense or time has been spared to have them excel all others in design, workmanship, and finish. These results could not be achieved were it not for the fact that we manufacture in our own works and by our own workmen every part entering into the construction of the "Toledo" excepting tires, horns, cyclometers, and like equipment.*
>
> *The speed of the engine is controlled by throttling, there being a hand lever fitted to the steering column, to advance or retard spark, and the*

accelerator throttles the mixture. In this manner, the operator can easily drive his machine from 5 to 35 miles per hour, simply be advancing or retarding the spark lever and placing foot upon the accelerator which is conveniently located.

According to Toledo's Attic, "When Secretary of State Elihu Root needed automobiles to carry Russian and Japanese diplomats around Portsmouth,

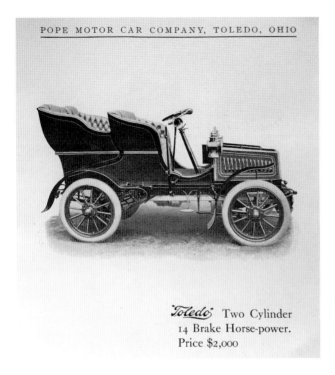

POPE MOTOR CAR COMPANY, TOLEDO, OHIO

Toledo Two Cylinder
14 Brake Horse-power.
Price $2,000

Pope-Toledo brochure. "Toledo Two Cylinder, 14 Break Horse-power. Price $2,000." *Paul Wohlfarth.*

New Hampshire, during the important negotiations that ended the Russo-Japanese War, he ordered a dozen Pope-Toledos."

Pope-Toledo began making other headlines, winning fifteen races and placing in twenty-nine others and becoming the first gas auto to climb Mount Washington. Pope-Toledo cars quickly increased in size and price, culminating in the fifty-horsepower limousine in 1907, sold for $6,000.

"While cars like the Pope-Toledo were beautifully built and returned excellent performance, the market was crowded and only a finite number of buyers could afford such extravagant motorcars," reads Stahl's Auto Website. By 1909, Pope-Toledo had gone into receivership, and only a few of the vehicles have survived.

INDUSTRY

BARCELONA-WESTFIELD FISHING INDUSTRY

In a stretch of dramatic Lake Erie waterfront, with forty-foot-high rocky bluffs, sits Barcelona, where the cliffs dip down to a long curving beach.

This popular spot for swimming and fishing began as a prime trade route for Native Americans, called the Portage Trail, going from Barcelona to Chautauqua Lake. In the 1700s, the French built a wagon road, and the first settlers moved in and built a gristmill on the Chautauqua River, according to an article by Larry Beahan on WestfieldNY.com. The opening of the Erie Canal made Barcelona an important link in the nation's westward surge. "The first steamboat arrived in 1818. Two boats, the *Fashion* and the *Diamond*, established regular steamboat service to the developing port," wrote Beahan.

About a decade later, the Barcelona Lighthouse was built to guide ships into the harbor (and remains today), and the Barcelona Inn was constructed, lasting until it burned down in 1961. "Warehouses, stores and fishing camps grew up along the shore as Barcelona became a thriving commercial fishing port in the early 19th century. Sailing vessels caught whitefish, herring, bass, and 50-pound sturgeon," wrote Beahan.

Fishermen even sold whitefish to hotels and restaurants in New York City. Westfield Fisheries, which opened in the 1940s, just down the hill from N.Y. State Route 5, is still there selling its legendary smoked whitefish. According to a *Buffalo News* article by Brian Hayden, it's the last fish market of its kind along the Lake Erie shoreline in New York that sources its products directly from those waters.

Fishing nets on Lake Erie at Barcelona in Westfield, New York. *Author's collection.*

The area has changed drastically since it opened, with restaurants replacing the fish markets. According to Hayden, "New regulations over the decades restricted catching walleye, whitefish and other species for commercial sale, and helped lead to the demise of a number of fish markets from Dunkirk to Erie."

Westfield Fisheries remains one of the only vendors between Barcelona and Michigan selling smoked whitefish, drawing in customers from hours away.

ASHTABULA HARBOR

"Ashtabula" in Algonquian means "river of many fish," but fishing wasn't the only thing the harbor town of Ashtabula was known for. More than sixty ships were built there between 1814 and 1868, and since so many were destroyed in storms, the harbor was said to be cursed, according to Carl E. Feather in *Ashtabula Harbor, Ohio: A History of the World's Greatest Iron Ore Receiving Port.*

A sloop named *Tempest*, launched in 1814, was involved in the salt trade between Ashtabula, Buffalo and Detroit, typically carrying 250 barrels along the route. Just weeks after being launched, it was detained at Buffalo, pressed into service of the U.S. government and unloaded of its cargo, according to Feather. The *Tempest*'s captain, crew and owners were detained for more than a week before they were released, but eleven more days passed before its twenty-five barrels of bulk commodities could continue their journey.

"Worse, in the course of its voyage from Buffalo to Ashtabula, the vessel ran into severe weather and sank on a sandbar off Erie, PA. The sailors were saved, but the schooner and all cargo were lost," wrote Feather.

Another ship, the *Hubbard*, built in Ashtabula in 1832, had two masts and was seventy-two feet long with a twenty-foot beam. It sank in a storm on November 22, 1842, and all passengers aboard died.

The harbor town also became known for its role in another major industry. In its heyday, more iron ore was said to go through Ashtabula Harbor than any other port in the world. "The port first claimed this distinction in the early 1890s and held onto the title for a quarter of a century, besting even the mighty ports of Cleveland and Toledo, Ohio," wrote Feather. "Eventually the port would capitulate not to Cleveland, but its neighbor to the east, Conneaut, for receiving the most tons of ore annually."

Entrance to Ashtabula Harbor, circa 1900. *Library of Congress.*

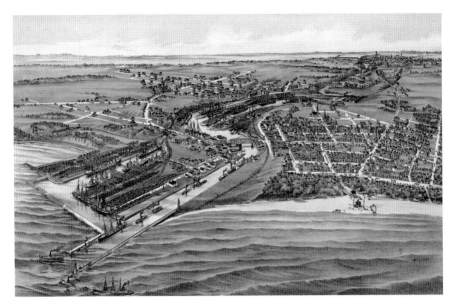

Ashtabula Harbor, 1896. *Library of Congress.*

According to Feather, in 1888 the mayor of Ashtabula, Colonel William C. Haskell, described the city as employing more than 1,500 people at miles of docks, dotted with expansive and modern machinery, "used by the two largest railroad interests in the country, giving business to the largest class of vessels on the lakes, that are pleased to trade at our harbor because of good depth of water and the splendid facilities for handling their cargoes."

The harbor was dug out manually because the channel that meandered through the swamp where the Ashtabula River met the lake was too shallow, narrow and twisting. Feather noted that it was constantly being modified and expanded to accommodate the huge ships that came through.

It was still a busy port even into the 1960s, when it was the third-largest iron ore port in the world. After decades of booming business, several changes played into the demise of the great coal and ore era, including environmental restrictions, the economy and improvements in bulk material unloading.

HULETT ORE UNLOADERS

Tall, steel machinery with hulking frames, connected to a clamshell bucket, once stood at various Lake Erie ports. The Hulett Ore Unloader has been compared to that of a mechanical dinosaur or steel grasshopper.

The machines revolutionized the iron ore shipping industry across the Great Lakes. It all started in the 1890s with a prototype designed and patented by Conneaut native George H. Hulett. He was born in 1846, lived in Conneaut until he was twelve and then moved to Cleveland. According to Case Western Reserve University (CWRU) Encyclopedia of Cleveland History, for almost two decades Hulett operated a general store in Unionville (east of Cleveland) before going back to Cleveland to work in the produce and commission business and then manufacturing coal and ore handling machinery. In 1898, while construction engineer with Variety Iron Works, he invented the unloader, and by the next year, his experiment was at Conneaut Harbor.

His employer at the time, Webster, Camp, & Lane Company of Akron, which built the prototype, reached an agreement with Andrew Carnegie, an industrialist known for leading the expansion of the steel industry, to install

Hulett ore unloader unloading a lake freighter in Cleveland at Pennsylvania Railroad iron ore docks, 1943. *Photo by Jack Delano, Library of Congress.*

Conneaut Harbor, 1901. *Library of Congress.*

one of the 1,500-ton machines on the Conneaut dock, with the condition that he would buy it if it saved money and labor; otherwise, it would need to be removed. It was a huge financial risk.

According to Carl E. Feather in a 2012 *Star Beacon* article, at first none of the dock workers wanted to ride inside the cage to descend into the hold, with the twenty-four-foot jaws wide open and ready to take a first bite of ore. Someone finally volunteered and took the first step to end an era of manual dock work.

"Rising 92 feet above the rail tracks, the steam-belching contraption's most notable feature was its vertical, articulating arm, at the lower end of which was a modified clamshell bucket capable of descending into the hold of a Great Lakes ship," wrote Feather. "An operator stood in a metal cage just above the bucket and thereby controlled the clamshell's movements. A second operator was on the machinery's carriage and controlled the travel of the machine along the dock."

Ore, which is essential to produce steel, once formed about one-third of trade on the Great Lakes and became one of America's greatest industries. It was discovered in the Lake Superior region in 1844 and made it to processing mills across the Great Lakes. "Construction of a canal around the rapids at Saul St. Marie, Mich., in the mid-1850s facilitated the movement of ore from the Upper Peninsula into the rest of the Great Lakes system," noted Feather. "In 1854, a 1,000-ton shipment of ore that was mined and hauled to the dock by an old gray horse and French car was loaded onto three vessels, one of them the *Sam Ward*, named in honor of the Great Lakes shipping magnate who got his start in Conneaut."

Feather added, "The huge challenge facing the dock workers was lifting this ore out of a ship's hold and into wheelbarrows on the vessel's deck. The laborers built platforms inside the holds and laboriously shoveled the ore from level to level until it reached the deck."

Carnegie not only bought the prototype but also ordered two more for the dock. Five steam-powered Huletts were installed: two at Conneaut, two at

Hanna's ore plant, Erie, Pennsylvania, circa 1905. *Library of Congress.*

Buffalo and one at Huron. Some electrical Huletts were built but consumed so much power that they often required their own powerhouse at the docks, noted Feathers. And when they were connected to municipal systems, the town's lights often dimmed when they were operating.

"Whereas formerly 100 men worked 12 hours to unload 5,000 tons of ore, 4 Hulett unloaders could unload 10,000 tons in less than 5 hours, requiring only 25 men. The unloader became universally used," reads a CWRU article about George H. Hulett.

"The Huletts revolutionized the unloading process by reducing the time needed to empty a 600-foot freighter, such as the steamship *William G. Mather,* from a whole week to half a day," according to a CWRU article on the Hulett Ore Unloaders. "The Huletts played a crucial role in Cleveland's ascendancy as a world leader of steel production and it is estimated that they unloaded some 100 million tons of material in their years of service."

Eighty Hulett unloading machines were built between 1898 and 1960, with Lake Erie and Michigan ports accounting for all but six of them on the Great Lakes. By the 1970s, more efficient self-loading freighters, requiring

View from above a Hulett ore unloader unloading a lake freighter in Cleveland at
Pennsylvania Railroad iron ore docks, 1943. *Photo by Jack Delano, Library of Congress.*

a smaller footprint, had replaced the Huletts, and most were scrapped.
"By 1992, only nine Huletts were still working around the lakes—four on
Whiskey Island in Cleveland and five at Conneaut. The Conneaut machines
were idle that year, while the Cleveland Huletts unloaded only 30 cargoes
during the entire season," wrote Feathers.

After eight decades in service, the last four Hulett Ore Unloaders at
the Cleveland Bulk Terminal on Whiskey Island fell silent at the end of
the 1992 shipping season. According to a CWRU Hulett Ore Unloaders
article, competing interest groups began debating their future. Conrail and
Cleveland-Cuyahoga County Port Authority wanted to demolish them to

make the Whiskey Island dock more efficient, but historic preservationists, led by the North Cuyahoga Valley Corridor group, believed that the Huletts had historic significance.

They received recognition for years of hard work when the Cleveland City Council granted them landmark status in 1993, and the American Society of Mechanical Engineers recognized them as a Historic Mechanical Engineering Landmark. In 1999, business and preservation groups reached a compromise: the four remaining Huletts would be dismantled—two sold for scrap and two stored on Whiskey Island—until funding was secured to move them to an appropriate site for reassembly and display. Decades later, the disassembled Huletts remain on Whiskey Island. A small piece of a Hulett is displayed at Point Park, at the end of Walnut Boulevard, in Ashtabula.

KELLEY ISLAND LIME AND TRANSPORT COMPANY

Island time begins as soon as you step on board the ferry that takes visitors and locals to Kelleys Island, about four miles north of Marblehead, Ohio.

The view of the historic Marblehead Lighthouse receding, the mass of land ahead getting larger and the rhythmic waves all help passengers disengage from the hustle and bustle of the "mainland." Cars are allowed on Kelleys Island, and while many bring them on the ferry, they sure aren't necessary to travel around the four-by-two-mile island, which is the largest freshwater American island on Lake Erie. Renting a golf cart, riding a bike or walking will do just fine.

According to the Kelleys Island Chamber of Commerce, it was named after brothers Datus and Irad Kelley from Cleveland, who were looking for an investment opportunity and found it in Cunningham's Island, as it was known in the early 1800s.

The Kelley brothers were drawn to the island's dense red cedar forest (prized steamboat fuel) along with the small quarry on the island's north side. By 1833, the Kelleys had begun buying the island's parcels of land, and by 1840, the name Kelley's Island was formalized when it became a township and later a village. (Over the years, the apostrophe has been dropped.)

According to Kelleysisland.com, only 150 people live on the island year-round, increasing to about 1,500 in the summer months. For decades, it's mainly been a vacation spot, catering to tourists, but before that it held an important role in another Lake Erie industry.

Lake Erie at sunset. *Photo by author.*

One of the most popular sites to visit on the island are the impressive glacial grooves, which are four hundred feet long, thirty-five feet wide and up to fifteen feet deep, according to the Kelleys Island Chamber of Commerce. This National Natural Landmark, created by slow-moving glaciers that carved the Great Lakes and Lake Erie Islands, draws people from around the world, but many don't realize that the island used to have even larger glacial grooves. "They were destroyed by quarrying operations and hauled down to lake freighters by a fleet of narrow-gauge Shays in the service of the Kelley Island Lime and Transport Co., reportedly the world's largest owner of Shay locomotives," according to Lee Rainey's 1986 *Railroad Model Craftsman* article.

The Shay was a steam locomotive that could operate on nearly any kind of track and helped transport limestone on Kelleys Island during its quarrying days, according to American-rails.com. At one time, limestone was one of the primary articles of commerce along the Great Lakes, behind coal, iron, stone and grain. By 1942, lake shipments of limestone were as high as 16 million tons, according to Rainey.

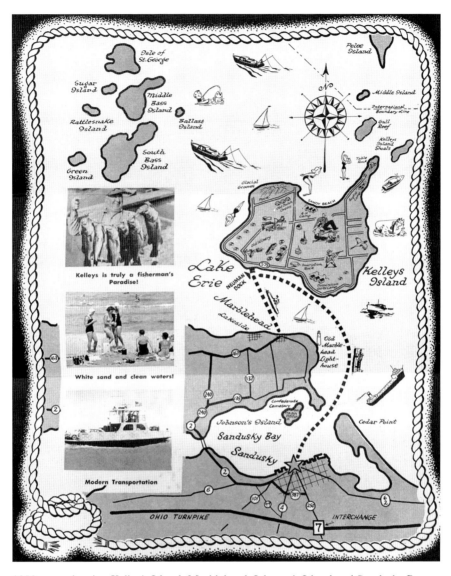

1950s map showing Kelley's Island, Marblehead, Johnson's Island and Sandusky Bay. *Patrice Kihlken.*

"Limestone and lime products served a variety of uses. Most important was the fluxstone produced for the iron and steel industry. Large quantities of building stone were handled in the earlier years, and lime for agriculture purposes was shipped throughout the Midwest. Naturally, railroads were essential to move the limestone products to the lakeside docks."

The first quarry opened on the North Bay of Kelleys Island in 1833. More than twenty years later, the first railroad was built on the island, only five hundred feet long and running from quarry to dock on the island's south side. "The tram was operated by gravity on the outbound trip and horses were used to haul back the empty cars," reads Rainey's article. "In 1886, the Kelley Island Lime and Transport Company [KIL&T] was chartered to consolidate all the quarries on the island. Eventually the KIL&T Co. was to control over 1,150 of the islands 2,888 acres."

In the early days, the North Bay plant was the most important of the KIL&T operations. By the early 1900s, it had a daily capacity of fifty-six tons and five hundred men and fifty horses working at the quarry, kilns, wharf and cooper shop.

The limestone was broken into layers, according to Rainey. At the top, often as little as thirty inches below the surface, was four feet of a bluish stone known as the extra cap, which was crushed and used to build roads. Below that was nine feet of bluish-gray cap rock, which was used for flux, and then six feet of building stone underneath that was burned for lime or sold as stone blocks up to five feet thick. The lighter gray bottom rock extended below the lake level and was used for lime burning.

"From the quarry, stone moved by rail to the crusher, a large L-shaped four-story structure. The crusher broke the stone so that it was no larger than five inches and no smaller than two, the optimum size for lime burning. It was then conveyed to concrete bins, from which it was dumped into rail cars on a pair of loading tracks," reads Rainey's article. "Next the crushed stone travelled to the kilns. Since these were charged from the top, the plant was built on the sloping shore of the lake. A stone ramp and timber trestle elevated the track to the height of the adjacent wharf, and switchback on the wharf swung the track into position on a long wooden unloading platform on the lake side of the kilns. There shovelers unloaded the cars into the kilns."

There was a small company with a large store and office building near the kilns, but it closed in 1909 and moved to mainland facilities. Several other quarries were developed in the south and west. The peak year was 1923, when 576,980 tons were loaded with 663 vessels stopping at the island. The following year, the south and west quarries were combined and extended a mile across.

Then in 1930, quarry activities extended to the center of the island. However, the market for building stone decreased and the island quarries closed in 1940. "The railroad equipment and loading shovels were cut up on the dock in 1941, and the West Bay dock was partially dismantled," wrote Rainey.

The Kelley Island Lime & Transport Company dissolved in the mid-1960s, and the last quarry on the island closed in 2007.

PEERLESS CHAMPAGNE COMPANY

The Lake Erie coastline and islands are known for excellent soil and a unique micro-climate for growing crops, particularly grapes. It's close to the same latitude as Tuscany, Italy, and a fifty-mile-long section known as the Wine Trail, including thirty thousand acres of vineyards along western New York and Pennsylvania, is nicknamed "America's Grape Country."

One of the most unique grape growing spots on Lake Erie is North Bass Island, also known as Isle St. George. It's a designated American Viticultural Area (AVA), meaning that it's a specified grape growing region requiring that at least 85 percent of those grapes make up wine produced there.

It's the only island appellation in North America, and Firelands Winery is the only winery currently leasing land on it from the Ohio State Parks Department.

According to SamCooks.com, Ohio winemaking began even before Nicholas Longworth, often called the "Father of American Grape Culture," planted Catawba grapes in the Ohio Valley in 1803. "The sturdiness of Catawba and its popularity in light, semi-sweet wines as well as in America's first sparkling wine, helped to make Ohio the leading wine-producing state by 1860," according to the site. "However, extremely humid conditions in the Ohio Valley led to widespread crop diseases, such as black rot and mildew. Combined with a lack of manpower after the end of the Civil War, this caused the decline of wine making in southern Ohio."

But it led to a rise in winemaking in northern Ohio as grape growers and winemakers headed to Lake Erie's shores to take advantage of the "lake effect"—lake breezes and a longer growing season thanks to warm lake water, even into late fall.

Since wild grapes grew on North Bass Island, growers were confident that grapes like Catawba, Concord and Delaware would thrive there. They were right, and wine production flourished between the late 1880s and start of Prohibition in 1920, with thirty wineries in the Sandusky area and seven on North Bass Island.

Rudolph Siefield was one of the grape growers who saw the island's potential. He was born on July 15, 1858, near Oak Harbor, Ohio, to parents who were German immigrants. His father died of malaria when he was very young, and his mother died a few years later. But he was resourceful and determined to make it on his own. According to a blog on MiddleBass2.org, referencing the 1917 *History of Northwest Ohio* by Nevin O. Winter, Siefield found work on Catawba Island and then Put-in-Bay. In 1875, he went to North Bass, where he worked at his brother-in-law's fishery for a decade. He saved his money to rent land, as well as the vineyard on it. He also bought the fish business and ran it, along with the winery, until he sold it to the Sandusky Fish Company.

"In the meanwhile Mr. Siefield had been buying land, his shrewd business instinct leading him to invest on the north shore of North Bass, continuing to add to his acreage from time to time, and he now has a home farm of fifty-two acres, thirty of which are in grapes," wrote Winter.

Siefield then became the owner and operator of the Peerless Champagne Company, growing Catawba grapes and producing "a grade of champagne which in flavor, appearance and bouquet cannot be distinguished from the finest imported wines."

Siefield also served in leadership roles in several organizations, including the Bass Islands Vineyards Company of Sandusky, which was a large producer of grape juice and the Becker Wine Company.

Siefield fell in love with his future wife, Nana Fox from Put-in-Bay, and they were married and had three children: Florence, Ida and Walter, all of whom they raised on the island. His children grew up, and his daughters married businessmen on Put-in-Bay. Walter, a graduate of the Sandusky Business College and the Ohio State University, married Rose Lescheid on June 13, 1914.

However, his marriage was tragically cut short. His story was included in a sequel to Winter's book, which was added in 2003 by Robin Burris-Cadez, who grew up on North Bass Island. According to Burris-Cadez, the Siefield family had lived in a white house, with a front porch, at the northern end of the airstrip, and Rose lived in a blue house across the road. After the wedding ceremony, some of their guests were sitting on the front porch, and Walter was leaning against a rail. The men had brought their rifles to perform a gun salute for the bride and groom and had them propped in various locations on that same front porch.

"A gentleman named Buttons Wires was sitting in a chair and his gun was behind him leaning against the side of the house," explained Burris-Cadez.

"He went to scoot back in his chair and in doing so knocked his gun over and it went off accidentally shooting Walter." Walter died a week later. Rose, who was clearly devastated, and her family left the island soon after.

The church was deemed bad luck, and no one got married there again until the 1960s. (There have been many happy weddings since then, including Burris-Cadez's.) Then, one day around 1979, Burris-Cadez's mom received a phone call from a gentleman who said that his great-grandmother lived on the island until 1914 and had never been back. He wanted to know if he could return with her to see the island one last time since she was ninety years old. Her mother happily agreed and offered them a car when they arrived. It turned out that the woman who was returning was Rose.

"They came in the fall when the grapes were ripe, which is when she wanted to come so she could smell the sweetness in the air given off by the sun ripened grapes," reads the sequel. Perhaps it reminded her of happier times, before her life was ripped apart by the loss of her young husband.

Today, very few people live on the remote island, which can only be accessed by private boat or plane.

HENRY FORD AND THE START OF PROHIBITION

A young Henry Ford built his first car, the "Quadricycle," and drove it around the streets of Detroit in 1896. Residents were flabbergasted by this "horseless carriage."

According to David Frew's *Midnight Herring: Prohibition and Rum Running on Lake Erie*, "The Quadricycle was only 45 inches wide, 43 inches high, and 79 inches long and yet it set the stage for the beginning of motor transportation and for Detroit to become the industry's epicenter." It not only led to Detroit's eventual nickname, "Motor City," but also played a role in the start of Prohibition.

Henry Ford, one of the world's richest and most powerful men, often argued that working men were not of sufficiently staunch "breeding" to tolerate alcohol consumption. According to Frew, his advisors told him that bars were popping up in the areas surrounding his factory, and his workers were gathering at these establishments to drink alcoholic beverages after their shifts.

Many of these men who assembled cars previously resisted working on an assembly line to mass-produce vehicles, taking away their skill as artisans and craftsmen. "Frustrated men left every day at 4:30 P.M. and headed

Henry Ford, 1927. *Courtesy Library of Congress.*

for their favorite taverns," wrote Frew. "Once inside the sanctuary of the pub, the agitation of the assembly line became fodder for discussion." Ford saw bars as a threat in fulfilling that purpose to revolutionize automobile manufacturing. "[He] imagined himself a social revolutionary whose role was to provide personal transportation for the masses."

Ford and his agents wanted to build social acceptance for the industrialization of Detroit and mold compliant factory workers, so he painted an idealized picture of fathers who dutifully earned a living working at his factory.

However, wives complained that their husbands were leaving at 6:00 a.m. and returning exhausted twelve hours later, implying that Ford and his colleagues were greedy industrialists. Ford's people argued that the workday ended at 4:30 p.m. and that only one thing was keeping them from returning home early: alcohol.

"In the hands of the working class, Ford imagined it to be the single biggest threat to his industrial vision," wrote Frew. "Taverns were luring workers away from their families, stealing precious time from children and fomenting company disloyalty."

Ford created an unsuccessful campaign to pressure men to go home right after work. Then, in 1916, he and some friends came up with a solution: outlaw alcohol, along with neighborhood bars and unions.

Many thought that his views were too extreme, envisioning dry social gatherings and parties, but Ford found a second group with a similar opinion: the Woman's Christian Temperance Union (WCTU), at the forefront of the emerging women's movement. The WCTU also felt that alcohol was destructive and contributed to creating abusive husbands and fathers.

With the backing of the WCTU, Ford convinced the State of Michigan to enact a statewide prohibition of alcohol in 1918.

Tavern owners became creative and started importing alcohol from Ohio and Ontario. Since they couldn't sell drinks to their patrons, proprietors began charging admission. The drinks were "free," but pubs began giving tickets to see a blind pig, which is where the nickname for these establishments came from.

Ford's junior prohibition only lasted two years and failed to keep factory workers from drinking and going home late. He may have lost that small battle, but nationwide Prohibition was passed into law shortly after on January 16, 1920, with the Volstead Act.

"The prohibition acts passed by the United States and Ontario, areas bound by language, trade, British heritage and the longest unprotected border in the world, almost ensured smuggling," wrote Frew. "And the epicenter of the border in question was Lake Erie, water boundary stretching from Buffalo, New York to Sarnia, Ontario. The border between Ontario and the United States tempted people from Toronto, Hamilton, London, and Windsor to participate in a business that made thousands of ordinary Ontario citizens wealthy beyond their imaginations. In the United States an equal number of Americans from cities along

Lake Erie and the Detroit River also benefited. Fortunes were made in less than a decade."

In America, it wasn't illegal to drink alcoholic beverages, but it was illegal to buy, manufacture or sell them. Across the lake, the Canadian government didn't pass a prohibition law, but the province of Ontario passed the Liquor Control Act, which made it illegal to drink alcoholic beverages; however, it was legal to manufacture and sell them for export.

These opposing and yet complementary laws were a catalyst for many creative and illegal endeavors. During Prohibition, Ontario's distilleries grew from eighteen to almost one hundred, and Lake Erie became a corridor to carry products to American markets such as Detroit, Cleveland, Erie and Buffalo.

RUMRUNNING

Although rumrunning occurred at many points on the lake, some of the greatest activity took place down the Detroit River.

"Almost immediately after Prohibition became law in the United States, the river came alive with bootleggers," according to *Lake Erie Stories: Struggle and Survival on a Freshwater Ocean*, by Chad Fraser. "Although it's impossible to know for sure, three-quarters of the alcohol that entered the U.S. from Canada during the dry years is said to have come this way, earning the river the nickname the 'Windsor-Detroit Funnel.'"

The river was lined with plain sheds on docks where booze were hidden until it was smuggled across. The proximity of the Hiram Walker Distiller—on the Detroit shore in Walkerville, Ontario—didn't hurt, and twenty-four hours a day, speedboats, rowboats and steamers loaded with liquor crowded the river.

Rumrunners took any measure necessary to transport liquor and make money fast. There are even rumors of an underwater pipe and cable system running from Canada to Detroit that helped sneak in booze to American speakeasies and blind pigs, where rebellious patrons could enjoy it.

The Detroit River was less than a half mile wide at some points, and there were said to be dozens of drop-off points on the Windsor side to stockpile product. Along this stretch of shoreline, one of North America's most ruthless urban gangs had a stronghold on the U.S. shore: the Purple Gang, which started long before Prohibition and scared everyone, even reportedly the police.

Detroit skyline, 1929. *Library of Congress*.

Hiram Walker & Sons Distillery, Detroit River, circa 1915. *Library of Congress*.

The gang controlled a system of fast boats that moved illegal alcohol from Ontario to Detroit by crossing the Detroit or St. Clair Rivers. According to *Pirates of the Great Lakes*, "Throughout prohibition, The Purples were infamous for their use of violence to smuggle Canadian whiskey to Detroit's waterfront, even smuggling it as far north as Clare, Michigan and onto Chicago waterfronts."

"Prior to 1920, the Purples used small speedboats to patrol the rivers and armor-plated automobiles to prowl city streets looking for competitors who were trying to run booze into their territory," according to *Midnight Herring*. "When they encountered a competitor, they didn't negotiate. They opened fire. By 1922, the Detroit and St. Clair Rivers had become a modern version of the Wild West."

As alcohol made its way south from Canada, the profits increased dramatically. For example, an eight-dollar case of twelve bottles of Seagram whiskey could wholesale for sixty-five dollars on the American side. (The bottles of pure alcohol were often mixed with water and relabeled, increasing the profit.)

Rumrunners even transported alcohol in bitterly cold and vicious weather by building sleighs or putting chains on their car tires so they could drive across the frozen lake, often bringing planks of wood in case they needed to create makeshift bridges to drive across cracks in the ice.

In *Ohio Lighthouses*, a crew member on the rum boat the *Barrel* said that they had made 180 trips delivering whiskey to Toledo without any trouble until December 23, 1928:

> *We left Toledo for Canada, dodging drifting ice and traveling in daylight since all the Coast Guard boats were dry-docked for the winter. Reaching Canada, we loaded and returned past the Pelee Lighthouse on Christmas Day. All went well until we were about one mile from Toledo. We ran into a solid sheet of ice an inch thick a mile from shore. Believing that we could cut through it, we ran into it for about 100 feet and could go no further. We were stuck. The next day, we walked ashore, found a phone, and called the boys, telling them to come and bring sleds. We left the rum boat in the ice all winter.*

In the spring, they brought the *Barrel* to Port Clinton but didn't find any damage to its hull.

Lighthouses, like the Vermilion Lighthouse in Ohio, helped guide rumrunners to shore. It was an obvious choice for landings since it was situated in a small town, said to have only one policeman, one night watchman and 1,500 residents during the Prohibition years.

"At night, boats brought the illegal liquor up the river to be unloaded at farms," reads *Ohio Lighthouses*. "When this became risky, nightly rumrunners would have someone onshore light a fire on a beach or near a creek so the skipper could meet a rowboat or find his way into an inlet. Fishing boats brought cheap beer and speedboats brought whiskey from Leamington and Kingsville, Ontario, directly across Lake Erie."

Some old-timers, the book notes, said that every barn near the lake in Vermilion held whiskey from Canada and that icehouses, normally used for storing fish in the summer, were filled with liquor covered with mats of straw and sawdust for insulation. Some of the fishing companies in town even rented out their storage barns to make a few bucks.

During Prohibition, fortunes were made on both sides of the lake, and the roles of those involved were rationalized and romanticized. "The men who provided booze to a thirsty American market were largely seen as folk heroes," wrote Frew. "On the Canadian side where booze was obviously being sent to the United States market, distillers and deliverers were regarded as good businessmen who were taking advantage of ridiculous American laws."

MIDNIGHT HERRING

In the early 1900s, Captain "Cap" William Kolbe was a leader in the Lake Erie fishing industry. He was a fisherman who sent thousands of pounds of processed fish to Erie, Pennsylvania, to be sent out to cities across the country.

He helped bring a railroad line to Port Dover's fish docks so his fish could be distributed to Canadian markets. Suddenly, from 1919 to 1923, the lake's prized fish species, herring, declined from 11 million to 6 million pounds. Other fish also began declining, like whitefish and yellow and blue pickerel (pike).

The independent fishermen were hit hardest since many had loans to pay on tugs and equipment, and they were desperate for a way to make money. Many met with Kolbe at a Port Dover tavern and came up with an idea: why not haul a new kind of herring in their tugs?

"The kind in a bottle that rides in the bottom of fish totes covered with ice—'midnight herring,'" wrote Frew. "Kolbe had a lot more to lose than any of the independents. He was holding loans on dozens of tugs and two

Crate of fish from Port Dover, Ontario, 1940s. *Library of Congress.*

major processing businesses with equipment. It was easy for him to make up his mind. Especially since the plan seemed foolproof. Before he decided, Cap Kolbe took a tug ride across the lake to make informal inquiries in Erie. His investigations revealed an opportunity that seemed even more lucrative than the fish business itself."

Midnight herring runs began in 1923, as railroad cars filled with alcohol lined up along the Kolbe processing building on the Port Dover dock. Tugs pulled up and were loaded with up to fifty cases of booze.

Many of Port Dover's fishermen lost interest in fishing as they saw how profitable rumrunning was. Yet Kolbe understood that some fishing should be continued, at least to keep up with appearances, so he asked his company tugs to attach gill nets on their way back from midnight herring runs. The break from overfishing Lake Erie actually seemed to help the fish supply because the company tugs began reporting bigger catches.

During Prohibition, alcohol wasn't the only thing illegally transported across the border. James Joyce's book *Ulysses*, which had been banned in America (because of content deemed obscene), was still available in Canada, and author Ernest Hemingway convinced a friend to smuggle copies of the books across the Detroit River.

Joe Semple, a rumrunner from Erie, opened the Owls Club when Prohibition ended. It had slot machines in the basement and was promoted to Erie's elite. During World War II, he was served a glob of grease in place of butter when eating toast at a local tavern. He spit it out and asked the bartender where the real butter was. According to Frew, the bartender told Semple that if he brought his ration stamps next time, he would try to get him the real stuff.

Semple took matters into his own hands and headed to Port Dover with a crew the next morning, where he could get real butter from Ingersoll, Ontario, the dairy capital of North America at the time. After transporting the butter across the lake and ladling it into tubs for resale, he began distributing it to hungry Americans. "Reprising his old prohibition whisky route, Joe Semple delivered butter to bars, restaurants and taverns where the special tubs were sold at a huge profit to patrons who were amazed that real yellow butter was being served."

BUILDINGS AND NEIGHBORHOODS

CENTRAL WHARF

In the early 1800s, Buffalo, New York, became the starting point for the ambitious Erie Canal. It stretched to Albany and the Hudson River, linking it to New York City, which helped it become a dominant center of trade and commerce.

To accommodate for the early 570-foot rise in elevation from the river to Lake Erie, eighty-three locks and eighteen aqueducts were constructed, according to NewWorldEnclyclopedia.org. "Its history spanned a little over a half a century," according to John H. Conlin's on WesternNewYorkHeritage.com. "[R]oughly from the opening of the Erie Canal to the railroad's eclipse of the canal, paralleling the great movement westward of emigrants populating the mid-continent."

Immigrants swarmed the wharf daily, many from Germany, sleeping on their luggage hauled on canalboats and waiting for their opportunity to build a new life in America. Steamboats carried these immigrants westward on Lake Erie as little bands played joyous music at the ship's stern, celebrating the beginning of what was hoped to be a grand adventure.

The wharf stretched along the north side of the Buffalo River from Main Street west to Commercial Slip (connecting the canal with the river, which let out into the lake). It was an important business hub for Buffalo, as well as for the rest of the country. According to Conlin, no one lived on the wharf, and there wasn't much retail trade. It was purely a wholesale

View of Buffalo, New York, from Lake Erie, circa mid- to late 1800s. *Library of Congress.*

Buffalo Old Central Wharf, Front Street, west of Main Street, with Board of Trade building in center. The buildings were demolished in 1883 to make way for the Lackawanna freight sheds. *Reproduction by permission of the Buffalo & Erie County Public Library, Buffalo, New York.*

trade mart, with buildings containing offices, sail-lofts (where sails were made) and warehouses.

To transport freight cargo (including barrels of flour and "high wines," inexpensive liquor with a high alcohol content), horse teams needed space to navigate through first-story warehouses along the wharf, so buildings were constructed to accommodate this need. They were also built with stairs, every fifty or so feet, along the front of the building, leading to second-story wooden balconies that were fifteen feet wide, providing a view of the river and lakefront. Historian Frank Severance remarked, "On the upper balcony crowds of merchants and vessel-owners were wont to gather, to note the incoming of vessels, or the struggles of some craft in the ice floe of early spring."

At the height of activity, in the 1860s, the wharf was said to be as busy as any part of Main Street in downtown Buffalo. People crowded along the heavy plank dock during navigation season, and the Buffalo River ferryboat water taxis were continuously gathered along the water, moving in and out of the site.

"There were idlers and curiosity seekers there. Young boys and men alike went sightseeing there to be entertained by the noise and activity, listening to the shouts of sailors and wharf men operating creaking hoists and winches, skidding barrels and loading them onto long-tailed dray carts and horse-drawn wagons of every description," wrote Conlin. "The background noise was regularly punctuated by steam whistles, ship bells and the tooting of the canal boatman's horn."

For about a half a century, this concentrated site played a pivotal role in catapulting business, immigration and transportation. Conlin referenced historian Frank Severance's thoughts on the importance of the Old Central Wharf as a major landmark, stating that even tough businessmen became sentimental at its passing in 1883:

> *The old wharf had so long been the business home of many of these men that its destruction seemed to them little less than desecration. Some of them had begun work there as boys. As they got on in years they had advanced from clerks to partners, had established firms of their own.... Year after year they had seen the commerce of the port grow. Their own efforts had made it grow; they had created the greatness of Buffalo and were part of it. And old Central Wharf...had been the center of it all.*

CANAL STREET

Canal Street, which ran along the canal between Main and Erie Streets, including part of the Central Wharf, was a rough-and-tumble strip of land only two blocks long. The district was connected to the rest of Buffalo by foot and wagon bridges over the canals. Sailors often stopped there, and it came to be known as the "Wickedest Street in the World."

According to BuffaloStreets.com, an 1847 report published in the *Buffalo Republic* noted:

> *During the summer, the very worst class of people inhabiting this portion of the first ward, have been permitted to gather there in unusual numbers, publicly enacting the most disgusting scenes, rioting by day and reveling by night….If the canal could speak, and its waters cast up the hidden bodies of those who have doubtless come to an untimely end, its tale of horror would startle the public mind.*

It was said that in its heyday, there was a murder every day. According to Angela Keppel on BuffaloStreets.com, legends have been passed down of saloon owners who would serve a man a poisoned drink, steal his clothes and personal items and then dump his body in the canal.

The first "dive bar" was believed to have started on Canal Street at Dug's Dive, operated by William Douglas, who was a former slave; patrons had to "dive" into the bar by climbing down a set of steep, slippery steps leading from the towpath.

Maiden Lane was a street that ran alongside Commercial Street, intersecting with Canal Street, and got its name "from the early days of Buffalo when the young women said goodbye to their sailor sweethearts or welcomed them home from voyages."

Canal Street, also known as "The Hooks" after the cargo hooks used by dockworkers and longshoremen, was lined with bars and taverns to entertain the sailors and canal workers; gamblers, drunks and prostitutes quickly turned the area into a crime-ridden district. It was even referred to as the "infected district" due to the diseases running rampant.

The song "Buffalo Gals" has been traced back to John Hodges, who is believed to have written it in 1844, under the title "Lubly Fan." According to the Library of Congress, it was adapted to suit different audiences and locations, and just over a century later in 1947, it captured the hearts of moviegoers in the film *It's a Wonderful Life*. However, according to BuffaloStreets.com, it was based on the women of the canal district, including hundreds of women of "easy virtue."

When the Pan-American Exposition came to Buffalo in 1901, women arrived from New York City hoping to make money off Pan-Am visitors. "They planned to take the 'Buffalo Gals' out of their territory by bringing their worldliness to the area," wrote Keppel. "The ladies of Canal Street resented the NYC women, and joined forces and attacked the NYC women with clubs, knives and fists, chasing the NYC women out of Buffalo. The NYC women were escorted by police back to NYC on packet boats and trains."

The Erie Canal was deepened and shortened in 1895, and railroads were built that were much more efficient for transporting goods. The neighborhood gradually changed as immigrant families settled in the area. The "ladies of fancy ways" began moving to other parts of the city, which soon led to the demise of saloons.

Italians settled into the Canal District, escaping the high taxes and famine of Sicily. Between 1900 and 1910, the Italian population increased from six thousand to sixteen thousand. By 1909, Canal Street had been renamed Dante Place. People lived in three- and four-story brick buildings that were former brothels and hotels for canal workers.

Keppel wrote, "In 1890, one old hotel called Revere Block, originally designed to hold 100 guests, had 1,040 residents living in crammed conditions. Reports in other buildings included 18 families crammed into four rooms; 56 people sharing eight bedrooms."

Social work organizations tried to improve the unsanitary conditions. Mary Remington headed up a settlement house, called Remington Hall, at the corner of Erie and Canal Streets. She worked with First Presbyterian Church to reform what was considered one of the vilest tenements in Buffalo.

Remington, often referred to as "Mea Madre" by Italian immigrants, wrote letters for the men who couldn't write, delivered soup and tea to those who were sick, bailed neighbors out of jail and helped show more than one hundred women, who had kept brothels, an upstanding way of life.

Many immigrants worked as laborers, working construction on the Pan-American Exposition in the northern part of the city in 1901. There was even a Venice replica on the Expo's Midway, representing the many Italian immigrants.

As the immigrants worked and earned money, they gradually shifted out of the canal region, buying homes in the Lower West Side. "The paved streets, concrete sidewalks and trees of the Lower West Side was seen as an

The lakefront in Buffalo, New York, 1905. *Library of Congress.*

improvement from the manure filled cobblestones and wooden sidewalks of the Canal District," reads BuffaloStreets.com.

In the mid-1930s, a Dante Place resident lit a candle and went into the basement, leading to a natural gas explosion, lifting the building off its foundation and killing five people. It brought national attention to the area's poor conditions, which led to new legislation. The City of Buffalo worked to raze the dilapidated buildings, and a year after the explosion, more than 160 buildings were demolished.

According to BuffaloStreets.com, a 1950 *Buffalo Evening News* article reflected on the street's earlier days:

> *Along the streets are old house numbers—148, 156—corroded and painted over and beaten by the weather of a hundred years. There is the occasional iron rail across what was once a barroom window, to protect it from stumbling drunks and lolling roustabouts. These are the flotsam and jetsam of an era long gone—a rough and roistering era of hard men and fancy women, of the waterside of Buffalo when it was young and heady with liquor, laughter and love at voyage end. It was the days when the canaler could sing that "The Erie was a-risin', the gin was gettin' low, and*

I scarcely think we'll have a drink til we get to Buffalo." It was the days when the sailors, swinging off their brigs and barks and ready for a fight or frolic, could yell: "Canaler, canaler—you'll never grow rich; you'll die in the ditch."*

In the 1950s, Marine Drive replaced Dante Place, and since then, most of the Canal District has been vacant. The once bustling Central Wharf and Commercial Slip were covered in stone and parking areas. Revitalization began in the 1990s and has continued in phases since then, working to preserve the area's history, bring new life to the waterfront and restore Buffalo's economic growth. Canalside, which spans a twenty-acre section of the historic Canal District, draws visitors to hundreds of festivals and events each year.

HOTEL VICTORY

Vacationers flock to Put-in-Bay throughout the summer, staying for the day, and taking the ferry back in the evening, or overnight to enjoy the full beauty of a Lake Erie sunset and sunrise.

More than a century ago, an ornate and palatial hotel was the focal point of the island's tourism. Hotel Victory was once known as the world's largest summer resort hotel, accommodating up to 1,500 guests, which was 500 more than the Grand Hotel on Mackinac Island, Michigan. "Hotel Victory was a marvel of extravagance," reads *Ohio Lighthouses* by Pat and Wil O'Connell. "The main lobby had a seating capacity of 1,000 people, and an orchestra played music night and day. The great ballroom with electric lights was the scene of social dancing and parties."

Author William G. Krejci wrote in his book *Lost Put-in-Bay*:

> To say that the Hotel Victory was an imposing structure would be an understatement. It was built in the popular Queen Anne style, featuring many towers, dormers, gables, turrets and spires. There were no fewer than 2,500 windows and six thousand electric lights. It also exhibited multiple wraparound porches and verandas. The palatial island retreat boasted four floors of guest accommodations. The main hotel structure stood at five stories, with some of the towers reaching as high as eight stories into the air.

The hotel concept began in Toledo, where resort developer James K. Tillotson dreamed up an architectural masterpiece. According to Krejci, Tillotson's plan was to build a resort on a scale never seen on the Great Lakes.

In December 1887, Tillotson brought his plans to South Bass Island to share with a group of enthusiastic residents, and a committee was formed to secure investors (with initial estimates between $300,000 and $500,000). After the Put-in-Bay Hotel Company formed, funds were secured, and a location was chosen on the island's southeastern side, at today's Stone Cove in South Bass Island State Park.

Toledo architect Edward Oscar Fallis drafted the hotel blueprints, and Sandusky builder George Feick's construction company built it. According to Put-in-BayOnline.com, Feick had to assemble his own sawmill, dining hall and dorms for his seventy-five carpenters to complete the project.

The hotel's cornerstone was set on September 10, 1889. According to Krejci, the hotel was named for the seventy-sixth anniversary of Perry's victory at the Battle of Lake Erie. Put-in-BayOnline.com reads, "Ever since Commodore Perry stationed his fleet here in the harbor and defeated the

Hotel Victory, 1910. *Author's collection.*

British in the Battle of Lake Erie during the War of 1812, Put-in-Bay has symbolized freedom, joy, and peace."

Many sightseers visited the island after the war to attend celebrations and festivals commemorating that battle. However, they had to leave by nightfall because there weren't accommodations on the island until about fifty years after the war. Hotel Victory helped develop the island's reputation as a vacation destination.

Building the hotel was a big undertaking, and about four hundred people were said to work on the hotel at any given time. According to Put-in-BayOnline.com, "The hotel site covered 100 acres. Twenty-one acres were reserved for the hotel, while the remaining 79 were divided into 475 villa lots that were sold to interested parties."

Although it was still a few years away from completion, it started welcoming guests on June 29, 1892, according to *Lost Put-in-Bay*, with a formal grand opening two weeks later, with celebratory ceremonies, fireworks and a banquet. Many guests arrived by an electric railroad that brought them from the docks.

The hotel was considered the grandest in America and went beyond the initial budget, costing more than $1 million to construct (equivalent to $30 million today). The main building alone was six hundred feet long and three hundred feet wide and surrounded a courtyard. According to Put-in-BayOnline.com:

> *A giant lobby connected the main building to the dining room, kitchen, and the servants' living areas. The two dining rooms could serve 1,200 guests at once. The hotel featured a 30-foot-long bar where cocktails flowed late into the evening (and early morning). The estate featured 625 guest rooms and 80 private baths.*

The hotel also had multiple writing rooms, a billiard room, a post office, a telegraph office, a newsstand and the island's only long-distance phone service. It offered guests dental and doctors' officers, laundry and tailoring services and barbers and hairdressers on site.

The Hotel Victory grounds were equally impressive. Visitors could amble down a boardwalk to the Lake Erie shore, cross a rustic wooden bridge that spanned a ravine or relax beside a fountain at the focal point of the hotel's landscaping. At one point, visitors could even swim in a covered one-hundred-by-thirty-foot swimming pool called the Natatorium. According to Krejci, it was one of the first co-ed swimming pools in the

BUILDINGS AND NEIGHBORHOODS

Rustic bridge at Victory Park, Put-in-Bay, Ohio, 1906. *Author's collection.*

United States (it was then considered risqué to swim with members of the opposite gender).

The hotel was described in the 1913 *Sketches and Stories of the Lake Erie Islands*:

> *The grounds adjoining the hotel form a landscape garden which nature and art combine to beautify. Profuse but tasteful and exquisite floral decorations appear. Foliage plants and blooms of torrid richness blend with paler hues; while climbing the white walls and stone-pillared steps, masses of madeira, morning glory, nasturtium and woodbine spread a mantle of blossom-starred greenery.*

However, this opulence and grandeur would not last long. Two months after Hotel Victory's grand opening, the business struggled to pay for its extravagant expenses and was pushed into receivership. A few months later, the stock market crashed, and the hotel was forced to close. According to *Lost Put-in-Bay*, "Tillotson leased the hotel the following season but abruptly closed its doors on August 10, 1893. After being closed for two years, the Victory was sold in 1895 at auction to architect Edward Fallis, who was one of the only two bidders. Upon taking possession, the sections of the hotel that had remained incomplete at the grand opening were finally finished. The following February, Fallis sold the resort to John Darst and Lysander K. Parks, who reopened it in the spring of 1896."

More than a decade later, on August 5, 1907, a $2,000 twenty-two-foot-tall bronze and copper statue of the winged Goddess of Victory was unveiled on the hotel grounds. Oliver Hazard Perry III, grandson of Commodore Perry, whose triumph on Lake Erie the statue was dedicated to, was one of the guests who attended the unveiling.

Just a few years later, the hotel was struggling once again with declining popularity, and it closed in 1909. A decade later, it opened again, and business was returning to the famed hotel when disaster struck.

On the evening of August 14, 1919, a neighbor of the hotel noticed flames shooting out of the upper cupola in the building's northwest corner. Although they immediately called the hotel's front desk to tell them about the fire, it quickly spread, and they couldn't reach that portion of the building. "Guests and staff raced to remove personal belongings and furniture from the hotel and were seen carrying items out onto the front lawn," wrote Krejci. "Many of these items were later hauled off by looters."

Crowds gathered to watch the intense flames, rising more than one hundred feet into the air and seen as far away as Sandusky and Detroit. "Ashes were carried on westerly wind as far as Kelleys Island, some six miles

Hotel Victory fire, August 14, 1919. *Author's collection.*

away," noted Krejci. "One by one, each section of the grand hotel collapsed with a sigh and a crash, surrendering itself to its incendiary fate."

According to Put-in-BayOnline.com, the Put-in-Bay Fire Department prevented the fire from spreading across the island, but it continued to smolder for several days. "Old legend suspected investors of arson," reads the site. "But that theory was quickly discarded, as they didn't have much insurance [about $126,000]. The cause was assumed to be a faulty light wire, and damage estimates ranged up to $1 million."

All that was left of Hotel Victory was its foundation, which was cleared off the site a short while later. In the late 1930s, the State of Ohio took possession of the grounds and developed it into South Bass Island State Park, where a campground now exists. Several ruins remain there, including that of the Natatorium and the Victory pedestal. (The statue itself was collected in a World War II scrap drive and melted down.) According to *Lost Put-in-Bay*, interesting artifacts like flatware and doorknobs are sometimes discovered at the site. It's all that is left to remember the triumph and tragedy of a once legendary hotel.

IRONVILLE

Ironville was a community on the east bank of the Maumee River in East Toledo, built on grit and industry, surrounded by oil refineries and pig iron furnaces. According to a historical plaque near the site, it was considered Toledo's first area of heavy industrial development, with iron manufacturing, coal shipping, oil refining, shipbuilding and flour milling operations.

"When I was a kid, my dad used to drive us from Point Place down to Ironville and park in front of what we, my five brothers and myself, called the Steel Pieces," said Cindy Ferg, recalling the vivid memory from her childhood in the 1960s on the East Toledo Historical Society's Facebook page. "It was Interlake Iron and the process of red hot bricks (ingots?) of pig iron dropping into rail cars while water sizzled as they were quenched."

The factory workers lived in the neighborhood with their families, and those who once lived there recall a strong sense of community pride. Casey J. Pfeiffer, of Toledo, said that mostly European immigrants settled there to work in the shipyard or for the railroad, like her grandparents, who lived there in the late 1940s and early '50s, after migrating from Austria. "Most were very poor coming here from different countries to make a new start/better way of life for their families like my grandparents," explained

Pfeiffer. "My grandparents [Rudolf Pfeiffer and Josefa Pfeiffer] literally came here with just the clothes on their backs, a few seeds to plant a garden and their passports."

She said that her grandfather had family living in Ironville who took them in until they had saved enough money to buy their own home. He worked for the railroad and the shipyard, and her father, Joe Pfeiffer, worked for the shipyard in the '70s.

In an Ironville scrapbook, compiled by Ron Mauter and available through Toledo Lucas County Public Library, an early print mention (1836) by "Trustees" of the area describes the future Ironville site:

> *The undersigned offer for sale about 1,500 lots on this important site. It stands at the mouth of the Maumee River, near its junction with Lake Erie. The back country is wide and rich, and the channel which passes has been acknowledged by experienced navigators to be deep and broad enough for vessels of the largest tonnage. The establishment of Roads and Canals, as well as other public works, which are projected within its neighborhood, gives it extraordinary and marked advantages.*

A 1902 clipping included in the scrapbook notes that the first store, sawmill, post office and hotel were built in East Toledo in the mid-1800s, along with the "Lake shore rd."; for many years, the stockyards were the leading industry of the east side.

Nearly three decades later, in 1863, a Cleveland firm built a charcoal furnace in Ironville (inspiring the name "Ironville") called the Manhattan Iron Company, which faced the river and had extensive docks on the Maumee. It employed 150 men and turned out eighteen tons of pig iron daily, and it changed hands several times, including in 1870, when it operated as the Sunday Creek Iron and Coal Company, (nicknamed "Sunny Creek Iron and Coal Co.") according to a 1938 *Toledo Blade* article. A several-mile-long railroad was built into the forest east of Ironville to reach the wood for charcoal for use in smelting the iron ore.

Around the same time, a grocery store, sawmill and brickyard were built in Ironville, along with a stave and handle factory and a distillery. By 1883, the original furnace had been torn down, but more industry was to come.

In the early 1900s, Ironville had its own neighborhood park, Lincoln Place Park. A 1910 drawing in Mauter's scrapbook, re-created from photos, shows that it had swings, a merry-go-round, a sandbox, two bandstands and a croquet lawn.

There was an Ironville neighborhood home that acted as a central meeting place, along with a church and Ironville School, at the corner of Milliard and Tiffin Avenues. Through the years, other Ironville industries included a Traufler Basket Factory, Gilmore Ship Yards, Paragon Oil Refinery (later Gulf Oil) and Interlake Iron Corporation, located next to American Shipbuilding Company on the Maumee River on Front Street in East Toledo. Interlake was built in 1902 by Pickands Mather, originally as the Toledo Furnace Company, and was designed to be the most modern pig iron plant in the world, lasting through the 1970s.

Deana Kohler's grandparents lived in Ironville. Her grandpa Henry Kohler was born and raised there, and she recalled many conversations with him about his experiences there before he passed. "He was one of the last families to leave there when they forced the neighborhood out," explained Kohler. "I know my grandma loved living there. She talks of how the neighbors were more like extended family members. Neighborly, if you will, better describes it. Everyone always looked out for each other and was nice to each other."

Don Clark moved to Ironville with his family when he was in seventh grade. "It was more like a town unto itself rather than a part of Toledo," he

Boys with ice cream cart in Ironville, in front of Paul's gas station. *Don Clark.*

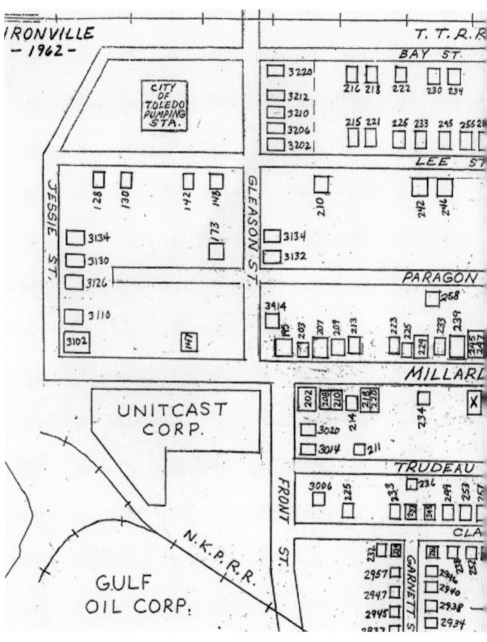

Rough map of Ironville, 1962. *Don Clark.*

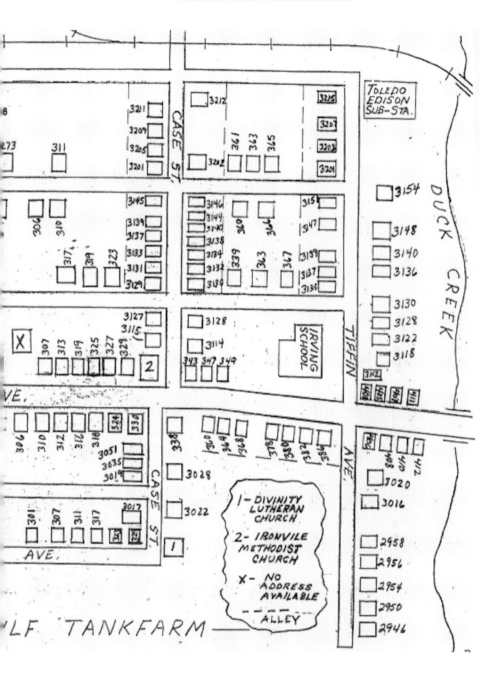

CARP-PAPRIKA STEW   Makes 6 servings.

1 lb. onion, peeled & chopped   3 green peppers, cleaned & chopped
2 T. lard   1 tsp. salt
2 T. Hungarian paprika   1 carp (or other freshwater fish),
3 lg. tomatoes, peeled & chopped   about 3 lbs. cut into lg. pieces

Sauté onions in lard until soft. Add paprika; cook 1 minute. Stir in tomatoes
and green peppers; cook about 5 minutes, until soft. Season with salt.
Arrange fish pieces in a saucepan and top with vegetables. Add just a little
water. Cook slow, covered, about 30 minutes, or until fork tender, adding
more water, if necessary. The gravy, however, should be thick.

23

Recipe for Carp-Paprika Stew, passed down from family to family in Ironville. *Don Clark.*

Don Clark's home being torn down in Ironville. *Don Clark.*

recalled. "The school was small enough that the custodian had two students stationed at the entrance whose job was to wipe the dirt and mud off of the student's shoes on a rainy or wintery day."

Clark said that a lot of the people who lived there worked at the Gulf Oil Refinery or the railroad (B&O). Some worked at the Unicast foundry. And church played a big part in people's lives, as was evidenced by two churches in such a small area.

For years, families lived in this community—kids of the workers became best friends, playing tag and makeshift baseball games in the street. They grew up, and many of them went on to work for the same companies their parents had worked for. Then in the 1960s, the City of Toledo purchased the community and homes, and everyone was forced to leave. They razed Ironville, with plans to build an industrial park. Clark said that his home was knocked down while he was away serving in the U.S. Air Force and he never had a chance to see it in person again.

The industrial park that was supposed to be built there never came to fruition, and Ironville became less than a ghost town—simply a memory of a once lively community that helped pave the way for industry in Toledo.

SHIPWRECKS AND LIGHTHOUSES

Shipwrecks were common on Lake Erie during the days of steamships for many reasons—the quick-to-change waters and dangerous storms, faulty construction and lack of regulations. In the mid-1800s, two steamers even both sank in the same spot, near Silver Creek, New York.

SS *GEORGE WASHINGTON*

The SS *George Washington* was a side-wheeled wooden steamship built around 1837 in Ashtabula. According to Silver Creek village historian Louis F. Pelletter, the ship's maiden voyage traveling from Buffalo to Cleveland took place on June 16, 1838.

In the 1820s, Silver Creek had a wharf extending 350 feet from the shore that was deep enough for vessels to load and unload cargo. Pelletter wrote that it became a very active shipping community with a warehouse and hotel, allowing farmers to ship their products, along with lumber potash and wood, to other Great Lakes ports.

Between 2:00 a.m. and 3:00 a.m., while three miles offshore Silver Creek, the *George Washington* caught on fire. Someone on shore noticed and rode on horseback throughout the community, yelling that a ship was on fire on the lake.

"Our community came to the rescue of the ship using boats that they had docked in the area," noted Pelletter. "It is thought that the fire started in the steam boiler area and spread very quickly. They attempted to steer towards shore, but the ship had wheel ropes for its steering mechanism which burned away causing the ship to be stranded. During this time period the wheel ropes were being replaced with iron rods to prevent them from burning off during a fire, stranding the ship. It was stated if this ship had these iron rods the outcome of this tragedy may have been different."

When people arrived, they took out boats to rescue people on the burning ship. The details are uncertain, but it's believed that about fifty people died during this wreck. The bodies of thirteen people were picked up that morning, and a funeral was held for them the next day. "The occasion was a very solemn and sad one," wrote Pelletter. "Although the subjects were all strangers, the entire community turned out to the funeral."

SS *ERIE*

Just four years later, in 1841, the SS *Erie* was headed to Chicago from Buffalo, carrying more than 300 passengers. That evening, there was an explosion, and the ship became engulfed in flames. According to Pelletter, about 250 people died in the fire, which happened at the same location as the *Washington* wreck.

This tragedy was one of the worst disasters on the Great Lakes and made international news since the immigrants had traveled across the Atlantic and down the Erie Canal and were on the last leg of their journey when disaster struck. The captain, who ordered his helmsman, Fuller, to steer for shore, died at his post trying to get the ship to Silver Creek Harbor, which led to his death being memorialized in poems and stories. For weeks after the wreck, bodies washed ashore and were buried in Silver Creek, Dunkirk and Sheridan.

The *Erie* sank about four miles from land in seventy feet of water and wasn't salvaged for fourteen years. A marker stands on shore near this site as a reminder of this devastating event, along with the positive changes it helped spur in the shipping industry.

ASHTABULA'S *TITANIC* SURVIVOR

Sometimes the direction of your life hinges on one moment—one fortuitous decision that changes everything. For Anna Sofia Turja, you could say that it was two moments. The one when she decided to board *Titanic* and the one when she decided to do everything in her power to get off.

Like many immigrants, eighteen-year-old Anna, of Finland, was drawn to America by the promise of a job and new beginning. Her half sister, Maria Lundi, lived in Ashtabula with Anna's brother-in-law, John, and her brother, Matt Turja, lived in nearby Conneaut.

According to an interview I conducted with her grandson Randy Lundi (whose father, Paul Jacob Lundi, was her son), her sister was working as a "domestic," and there was an opportunity for Anna to have a similar job, if only she could make her way to the States.

Randy said that Finns settled in Ashtabula, like other areas along the Great Lakes, because the climate and geography was like Finland and because they were fleeing the harsh political climate between Russia and Finland.

On April 3, 1912, Anna mailed a letter from the Finnish port of Hangö to her family in Ohio. According to EncyclopediaTitanica.org, she and one hundred other Finns were about to set sail to connect with *Titanic* in Southampton, England. Once aboard, she traveled in third class, sharing a room with three other women. She was not only traveling without family but also with a major language barrier—she didn't speak a word of English.

On the evening of April 14, she was awoken in her bed by a collision she described as a shudder. According to her grandson John Rudolph in a 2012 *Star Beacon* article, a crewman pounded on her cabin door, hollering emergency orders she didn't understand. A Finnish-speaking passenger explained, the ship was in distress and she should put on her life jacket and warm clothes. She later said, "We were not told what had happened, and had to do our own thinking."

The article says that at first, Anna and a group of Finnish immigrants went up to a deck to listen to the band play. "People were everywhere. Many were shouting," she said in a 1962 *Star Beacon* interview. "An older woman in our cabin, who had been my unofficial guardian, since I was 18 years old, panicked when she got up on deck. She urged me to a higher deck where it is safer. But I decided to go where the people were and went back down."

Randy said that the women thought they would be safer on the high point of the ship, but Anna decided to follow a porter who said to head downward. The highest point ended up breaking in half, dropping the women Anna had been with into the icy waters below.

Shelley Terry wrote in the *Star Beacon*, "That decision saved her life. A crew member grabbed her and shoved her into the third from last lifeboat, family members said." *Titanic* had sunk so low that Anna's lifeboat was launched right off the deck, while earlier lifeboats were lowered as many as seven stories from the deck to reach the water.

Her grandson said that when she talked about being in the lifeboat, it wasn't the cold that stood out but rather the stillness and darkness. John said she told stories about burning anything they could, even money, to signal the other lifeboats to stay together. As she sat in the lifeboat, she described the sound of boilers exploding on *Titanic*, sending waves through the water that rocked the lifeboats as they pulled away. They tried to quickly get far away from *Titanic* because the undertow, as it was sinking, was pulling everything down with it.

EncylcopediaTitanica.org details her memories: "The lifeboat was close to the *Titanic* when it sank. The moaning and calling for help were awful, she later described the cries in the water: 'finally it was almost like an hymn, you could hear' which continued for what she thought was two or three hours. She was told they couldn't go back to rescue swimmers because their boat was full."

However, Randy said his Mumma (pronounced "Moo-ma," which is Finn for grandma) talked about one of the most terrifying moments, when people in the water tried to grab onto her full lifeboat, tipping it. The oarsmen hit people with their oars to knock them back into the water so their boat wouldn't capsize.

By sunrise, Anna could see a dim ship on the horizon, the *Carpathia*, which rescued more than seven hundred survivors from lifeboats. After being transferred to *Carpathia*, a Finnish man told her that he had been in the water for six hours and claimed that some people were shooting at each other as *Titanic* sank; he narrowly escaped being shot for trying to get into a lifeboat lowering with ample room left in it.

Anna was one of 2,230 people who boarded *Titanic* and one of 714 to survive. In an April 2012 *Cleveland Plain Dealer* article about the 100th anniversary of the *Titanic*, writer Michael Sangiacomo interviewed her grandson Randy, who was still in awe of her survival, with so many odds against her. "Think of the way the world was in 1900s," Randy stated. "For the *Carpathia* [which rescued the people who made it off the *Titanic*] to be close enough to offer assistance is just amazing. My grandmother did not panic, and she made a single decision that saved her life."

When *Carpathia* reached shore, Anna and other survivors bypassed the usual stop for immigrants on Ellis Island and were taken to St. Vincent Hospital. She learned that her roommates had not survived, and everything she had, except the clothes on her back, were at the bottom of the sea. The

White Star Line paid for her hospital bill and train ticket to Ashtabula. She arrived aboard the Nickel Plate train and was greeted by her sister, brother and his brother-in-law, Emil Lundi.

According to Cleveland.com, a DVD made in 2011 by Anna's son, Martin Lundi, documents her incredible story of survival, including the time after, like when she met Emil for the first time: "Emil took one look at my mother and told his brother that he should not get used to having her around as a worker, because he was going to marry her. A year later, he did just that and became my father."

Anna never returned to Finland and never took the "domestic" job. Martin was one of seven children whom Anna and Emil had in the following years, raising them in Ashtabula on West Ninth Street. (Emil worked as chief custodian at Ashtabula Harbor High School for years, and as an adult, his son Paul worked on the shipping lines, as a steersman for Cleveland Cliffs and later at North American Rockwell. Other descendants became singers and entertainers and served in the military, like Randy.)

After picking her up at the station, her family took her to her sister's house at 81 Oak Street. The neighbors marveled at "the wisp of a girl they met." Her arrival created a media frenzy, and a newspaper reporter described her as "fair, slender, and exceedingly bashful."

Since Anna's name had been on the lost passengers list, her family in Finland thought that she died in the wreck, until six or so weeks later, when they received her letter saying that she was alive. According to Cleveland.com, Anna never truly escaped *Titanic*, at least not in her mind—every year journalists would ask her to talk about her memories. Her son said that she didn't like being in the spotlight but felt obligated to share the story to keep the memory of the tragedy alive. Randy said she told the stories to her children, who then shared them with others. She and her husband also refused to join in any lawsuits over the loss. "She and my grandfather felt they didn't need to go after money. Grandma had her life, and that was compensation enough."

In 1958, she was a guest at the premiere of the film about *Titanic*, *A Night to Remember*, playing at the Shea Theater, which once stood in Ashtabula. Her grandson said, "She was horrified at the depiction of death. She thought the Hollywood movie would have a happy ending where all the people were saved. When she figured out the movie was an accurate depiction of the night she lived through, she broke down crying."

It was the first movie she had ever seen, and according to EncyclopediaTitanica.org, her son interpreted for her while they watched

Anna Lundi next to her rose garden in Ashtabula, surrounded by family. *Randy Lundi.*

because she never became fluent in English. When the movie ended, as the story goes, she turned to her son with tears in her eyes and said, "If they were so close to take those pictures, why didn't someone help us?"

Her grandson John Rudolph said, "She always said she didn't know why God saved a poor Finnish girl when all those rich people died. She was a sweet, God-fearing woman." The tragedy was always a part of her life, but she never let it define her, instead focusing on the love for her family that came after the tragedy.

Her grandson Randy described her as a loving woman, with a warm, radiating smile, and a great cook who loved serving her family homemade recipes from their homeland, including nissua (Finnish coffee bread) and cinnamon rolls. "Everybody's got a purpose and our purpose now is to be so thankful to God for allowing her to live and create such a legacy of a faithful God-fearing family that we can pass on to generations and keep that memory alive for hopefully generations to come," Randy told me, his voice full of emotion for his beloved Mumma. "God has a purpose for every life. He has a purpose for every tragedy. He has a purpose for every disaster."

Anna lived to be eighty-nine years old and is buried at Edgewood Cemetery in Ashtabula. She has many descendants who carry on the story of *Titanic* for her, including a few still in Northeast Ohio. They share it so that her story of courage and bravery and the lives lost more than one hundred years ago will never be forgotten.

Note: Thank you to Karen Raisanen, who grew up in Ashtabula, the daughter of a dock worker from the harbor, for sharing Anna's story with your daughter, Northeast Ohio resident Joanne Abruzzino. And thank you, Joanne, for then sharing it with me.

CITY OF DRESDEN

Long Point, Ontario, often played a role in rumrunning during Prohibition, so it was common to see ships in the harbor. But it was uncommon to see the whiskey bottles, secretly carried on those ships, floating in Lake Erie and drifting onto the beaches. It happened one night, more than a century ago, when the propeller-driven steamer *City of Dresden* made an infamous arrival.

The ship was launched in Walkerville, Ontario, on the Detroit River near Windsor in 1872. Two years earlier, it became the home of Hiram Walker's distillery, the largest distillery in Canada.

A half century after its launch, *City of Dresden* was still cruising the waters of Lake Erie until it came to an end that seemed almost befitting considering the whiskey town from whence it came.

"On Nov. 18, 1922, a strong southwest gale pounded the upbound City of Dresden until her aging seams opened," according to a *Windsor Star* article by Cris Kohl. It sank in about thirty feet of water, just offshore Port Rowan, near Long Point. Captain J.E. McQueen, the ship's owner, and his five-man crew were able to climb into a lifeboat and fight the strong undertow to reach shore. However, the captain's twenty-one-year-old son died while trying to rescue an overboard crew member, who ended up surviving, wrote Kohl.

City of Dresden was said to be carrying a cargo of coal, but it soon became apparent that it was filled with whiskey. Women from nearby farms tried to help the struggling sailors reach shore in their lifeboats. One waded into the dangerous water to help secure the boat. All the while, the massive waves carried case after case of whiskey toward shore, causing a frenzied search-and-rescue mission among the local men. "Farmers fetched their horse-drawn wagons, and some their newfangled trucks, while others arrived on foot with sacks to gather up the liquor bottles," wrote Kohl. "Some individuals reportedly sat on the beach drinking single bottles they had recovered."

Nearly every bottle of the five hundred cases said to be on board was taken to homes or hidden in the marshlands for future retrieval. According to the article, an Ontario newspaper headline of the time may have had summed it up perfectly: "Woman Saves Lives of Crew While Men Salvage Liquor from Ill-fated Rum Runner."

When law enforcement arrived, nothing remained for them to seize except a few empty bottles. Dozens of local farmers were later summoned for police questioning, and a few were charged with liquor theft, based only on suspicion. When the police were unable to provide evidence, all charges were dropped.

According to Kohl, "In a 1972 newspaper article on the 50th anniversary of the sinking, many of the farmers' sons laughingly admitted their naughty dads had hidden considerable alcohol from the wrecked *City of Dresden* back in 1922."

KELLEY ISLAND

Ships played a pivotal role in the quarrying industry on Kelleys Island. In 1905, the Kelley Island Lime & Transport Company (KIL&T) owned several tugs and steamships, including the sandsucker *Kelley Island*.

Kelley Island delivering sand at the Cleveland builder supply company dock, 1938. *Cleveland Public Library.*

In 1925, Captain William G. Slackford, born near Sandusky in 1861, was the captain of the *Kelley Island* for six years, having sailed since he was seventeen. "He [Slackford] had previous command of popular steamers on the Cedar Point run, the *R.B. Hayes* and the *A. Wehrle Jr.*; thus Slackford lacked no sailing experience on Lake Erie," wrote Richard Gebhart in *Ships and Shipwrecks: Stories from the Great Lakes.*

Slackford and his wife, Hattie Andrews, had four children, and although he was a well-respected shipmaster, each time he headed out to sea there was a risk he wouldn't come back. Lake Erie is known for its treacherous water and winds, clocked near one hundred miles per hour. According to an article in *Railroad Model Craftsman* magazine, of the thirty-three vessels operated by the KIL&T over sixty-five years, six were lost on the lake while in service for the company.

On May 2, 1925, Slackford, on board the *Kelley Island* with his son William and a crew of sixteen men (including another father-and-son pair, Paul and Morton Everett) left the home port in Sandusky and headed into open water. Around 8:30 a.m., the *Kelley Island* arrived at its destination near Point Pelee, Ontario. "She dropped anchor and lowered her suction tube over the port side and began on her sand cargo," wrote Gebhart.

A few hours later, the *Kelley Island*'s sister ship, the *John M. McKerchey*, completed its load and noted that everything seemed fine on the *Kelley Island* before going back to Sandusky to unload its sand cargo.

Around 2:30 p.m., the vessel's two hoppers were full, and it was ready to head to the company's Cleveland dock. A boom was swung out to retrieve the suction pipe that had drawn the sand into the ship, and four crewmen prepared to secure a steel plate on the opening of the pipe. However, when the suction pipe was removed, the *Kelley Island* was quickly inundated with water.

According to the May 3, 1925 *Sandusky Register*, "While four men were valiantly fighting to fit the plate over the hole to stop the flow and save the vessel, one partition of the ship became filled. This caused a shifting of the sand cargo and that, together with the heavy seas running caused the capsizing."

Captain Slackford sounded the alarm in the pilothouse. Many of the men slipped from the capsized ship into the cold waters of Lake Erie and immediately drowned. Several grabbed on to the motionless propeller and overturned hull of the ship.

Deckhand Curtis Brown of Sandusky was hailed a hero because he rescued three crew members by grabbing a floating rope nearby and pulling them to the capsized ship. Survivors included Brown, Andrew Krause, William Loveridge and Scott Pethbridge, all of Sandusky; Clarence Bloomstrom and Nicholas Rennard, both of Toledo; and Morton Everett of Oak Harbor. They all huddled together in the frigid water hoping to be rescued, but according to Gebhart, they began to lose hope as three large steamers and a tug passed them by.

Later in the afternoon, the men were finally rescued, and survivor William Loveridge relayed the story to the *Sandusky Register* over "long distance telephone." "Loveridge with teeth chattering and wrapped in blankets, answered the telephone at the Point Pelee Lighthouse, where he and the six other survivors were quartered after being landed there by the *Flossie B.*, a [Canadian] fishing boat which came to their rescue two hours after the wreck occurred."

"'I was asleep in my bulk at the time the ship first began to sink,' Loveridge said. 'The warning whistle awoke me and I barely had time to get out of my bunk when the ship overturned completely.'"

According to the *Sandusky History* blog, "The *Sandusky Register* reported that several other crew members also heroically tried to save the ship from the water that was rushing in. Alvey Martin and Frederick Holder failed in their efforts. Captain Slackford remained in the deckhouse as the ship sank."

According to *Sandusky History*, nine men died in the disaster, including Captain Slackford, his son William, Oley Kriss, William Mayer, Rolland Will and Alvey Martin, all of Sandusky. Frederick Holder and Paul Everett, both of Oak Harbor, and Thomas Moran, of Castalia, also drowned.

A shipmaster's pennant that belonged to Captain Slackford is in the collections of the Follett House Museum in Sandusky.

CLEVELAND'S FIRST LIGHTHOUSES

It's hard to imagine while standing amid the tall buildings at the corner of West Ninth Street and Main Avenue, in downtown Cleveland, that a towering lighthouse once stood there.

In 1796, Moses Cleaveland and his surveyors with the Connecticut Land Company arrived at the mouth of the Cuyahoga River (in what would soon be called Cleaveland; the *a* was later dropped). Over several decades, as people settled in the region, the city evolved and became an important port city on Lake Erie. A light, guiding ships in and out, became a necessity, so in 1829 the first lighthouse was built on the hill at the north end of Water Street (now West Ninth) looking over the lake.

According to *Ohio Lighthouses*, Levi Johnson built the sixty-seven-foot rubble masonry lighthouse, with an iron lantern that burned whale oil and held thirteen patent lamps and fourteen-inch silvered reflectors along with the nearby two-room keeper's house.

At the time, the land looked much different. According to News5Cleveland.com, the shoreline started closer to where the Main Avenue Bridge is today, and the East Bank Flats, apartment buildings and bridge didn't exist. Also, the land Cleveland Browns Stadium sits on, and everything behind Cleveland City Hall, was created using landfill (as was Edgewater Park).

Then, around 1831, a scaffold-type tower was built on the six-hundred-foot-long pier on the east side of the entrance to the Cuyahoga River. The lighthouse keeper, Steven Woolverton, serviced both lights on the hill and the pier, which was replaced several decades later with a cast-iron structure with a sixth-order fixed lens.

Several years later, according to Ligthousefriends.com, Lieutenant Charles T. Platt, while surveying lights on Lake Erie, recommended the lighthouse on the bluff be discontinued, saying, "It is true that the light-house could be seen to a greater distance than the beacon, but the height of the adjacent coast, and the entire want of shoals or hidden rocks near by [*sic*], entirely obviate the necessity of a light conspicuous farther than the beacon."

By 1850, the beacon light on the pier had been rebuilt into an open-frame cast-iron tower, with a fixed light, until a fourth-order Fresnel lens was installed, flashing every seventy seconds. Since this fulfilled navigational needs at the entry to Cleveland, the hilltop light was discontinued until a few years later, when it was renovated and relighted, to confirm with an act of Congress, according to Lighthousefriends.com. A decade later, Congress appropriated funds to build a new lighthouse and keeper's dwelling at that same location. A temporary light was established so the old stone tower could be removed and new structures built.

Work was suspended on and off for various reasons, but the new Victorian Gothic–style lighthouse finally began operating with the opening of the 1873 navigation year. According to *Ohio Lighthouses*, it was one of the most elaborate in the country. Lighthousefriends.com says it was a "three-story dwelling and attached eighty-three-foot tower were built of brick and accented with stone trimmings."

Cleveland main lighthouse and keeper's house, southwest corner of Water Street (West Ninth Street), 1885. *Cleveland Public Library.*

Cleveland Harbor entrance, circa late 1800s/early 1900s. *Library of Congress.*

It was originally intended for two keepers but was renovated to provide additional quarters; by 1909, it had seventeen rooms. However, it served its role as a guide to ships for a short time. Although the lantern room held a three-and-a-half-order lens with a fixed white light, captains coming into the harbor couldn't see the beacon due to Cleveland's fog and industrial smoke.

In the late 1800s, it was discontinued, and the breakwater lighthouse took over serving as a beacon. A few years later, according to Lighthousefriends. com, "a fire broke out near the dwelling and excessive heat cracked seven panes of glass in the lantern room, killed the lawn, trees, and shrubbery on the lot."

Parts of the tower were removed—including the lantern room, iron stairway, lens and finished stone on the upper part of the tower—and were used to build the Braddock Point Lighthouse on Lake Ontario in New York. The rest of the tower was torn down, and material was used to build an addition on the west side of the keeper's house, which had grown to a colossal forty-three rooms to house four keepers and their families, who lived there until 1927.

A decade later, when the Main Avenue High Level Bridge was built, the keeper's dwellings were demolished. "In its removal," the Lake Carriers' Association commented, "there disappeared the last vestige of the imposing structures of architectural beauty that characterized Cleveland's Main Light for many years."

All that remains is a short wall connected to a set of sandstone steps, from the original lighthouse, leading up to a parking lot in downtown Cleveland.

It's likely that many passersby have wondered about those steps, and now, thanks to the nonprofit Downtown Cleveland Alliance, a new Lighthouse Park has been created to honor that important piece of maritime history.

According to an August 2022 *Cleveland Plain Dealer* article, the park's feature is a sculptural light bar that goes over the historic steps, representing the light of the old lighthouses, along with a plaque showing a picture of the lighthouse and its history. There's also a wraparound wooden seating area for walkers to rest and imagine the grandeur of the site all those years ago.

LOST VERMILION LIGHTHOUSE

The Vermilion River empties into Lake Erie after traveling through the city of Vermilion. It's a region rich with maritime history, from its role in rumrunning to harboring captains and sailors, giving it the nickname at one point "City of Sea Captains." From the mid-1800s to early 1900s, a lighthouse stood on the edge of the shoreline, beckoning to mariners.

Vermilion's harbor was growing, and by 1847, according to DiscoverVermilion.org, the people of Vermilion had constructed their own navigational aid: wooden stakes topped with oil-burning beacons at its entrance.

Congress appropriated $3,000 to build an actual lighthouse at the end of the pier, but it took a beating by the elements; by 1852, the lighthouse and pier needed $3,000 in repairs. Seven years later, in 1859, the lighthouse was rebuilt, and the new one was made of wood and topped with a whale oil lamp (oil rendered from whale blubber).

"The lamp's flame was surrounded by red glass, resulting in a red beam that, with the help of a sixth order Fresnel lens, was visible from Lake Erie," reads DiscoverVermilion.org. "A man from the town looked after the lighthouse, lighting the lamp each evening and refueling it each morning."

Although functional, it still wasn't sturdy enough to withstand the damaging wind and waves from the lake, so Congress appropriated funds to build a new lighthouse in 1866, this time out of iron on the west pier, designed by a government architect and cast by a company in Buffalo, according to DiscoverVermilion.org. "To cast the lighthouse, the ironworkers used sand molds of three tapering rings, octahedral in shape," reads the site. "The iron they used was from unpurchased Columbian smoothbore cannons, obsolete after the Battle of Fort Sumter. As noted by Vermilion native Ernest Wakefield, 'The iron, therefore, of the 1877 Vermilion lighthouse echoed and resonated with the terrible trauma of the War Between the States.'"

The lighthouse traveled from Buffalo in pieces on barges hauled by mules down the Erie Canal, taking two weeks to reach Oswego, New York. The materials were then transferred to the *Haze*, a steam-powered propeller vessel, which carried it west through the Welland Canal, where twenty-seven locks raised it to the water level of Port Colborne and then on to Lake Erie. It's unknown why such a tedious route was chosen when it seems it could have been transported directly across the lake. The *Haze* stopped in Cleveland to pick up the lighthouse's lantern and fifth-order Fresnel lens, lime and lumber to build its foundation and a crew of workers to raise the lighthouse.

After arriving in Vermilion, work began a day later. After the foundation was built and the lighthouse pieced together, it measured thirty-four feet tall, standing at the end of the pier with a four-hundred-foot-long catwalk running above it, allowing the keeper to travel above the dangerous waves. Over time, the lighthouse was moved closer to the end of the pier, where it survived multiple close calls with ships.

At the beginning of the Great Depression, Vermilion teenagers Theodore and Ernest Wakefield noticed that the lighthouse was leaning toward the river after a bad ice storm destroyed its foundation. The Wakefield boys told their dad, Commodore William Frederick Wakefield, who reported it to the U.S. Lighthouse Service in Cleveland. The lighthouse was determined to be unstable by the U.S. Army Corps of Engineers, and within a week it was dismantled. "Vermilion residents awoke to discover their lighthouse was gone," reads *Ohio Lighthouses*.

According to DiscoverVermilion.org, Commodore Wakefield offered to buy the lighthouse to move it to his property, Harbor View, but he was denied. Years later, in the 1990s, Wakefield's home was donated to Bowling Green State University and later sold to the Great Lakes Historical Society, becoming the main structure of its Inland Seas Maritime Museum. After a fundraising campaign, spearheaded by Ted Wakefield (one of the teenagers who originally noticed it leaning), $55,000 was raised to build a sixteen-foot replica of the lighthouse on the property. According to rumors, an 1877 gold

Vermilion lighthouse. *Author's collection.*

piece was placed under the vertex of the octahedron that would point true north. The lighthouse is still operating today as an active navigational aid.

For years, residents wondered about what happened to that original lighthouse. A few years after the new replica lighthouse was built, they found out. In 1994, after Olin W. Stevens, who had been the lighthouse keeper prior to 1929, died, his grandson found an old trunk filled with articles and memorabilia. A 1937 newspaper clipping from Jefferson County, New York, welcomed Stevens as the new lighthouse keeper for Charity Light, on Lake Ontario.

According to *Ohio Lighthouses*, "The article reads, 'Altho this is his first duty on Lake Ontario, Charity Shoal Light is an old friend. The tower was under Stevens's charge at Vermilion. Victim of an ice shove, it was salvaged and taken to Buffalo, where it was assigned to Charity.'"

His grandson brought the article to the Vermilion Museum, and after years of wondering, the people of Vermilion rejoiced in knowing that the lighthouse still existed as the East Charity Shoal Lighthouse, having the rare distinction of flashing its light on two different lakes.

RESTAURANTS AND RECREATION

HICKS ICE CREAM COMPANY

In a time when most African Americans weren't business owners, much less acknowledged as inventors, John S. Hicks managed to break the mold—and create one at the same time. He was the son of a former slave, born in Virginia in 1845, and began an ice cream business in Springfield, Massachusetts, before turning twenty years old.

According to an article by Jeff Sherry, museum educator at the Hagan History Center, in Erie, Pennsylvania, Hicks moved to Erie in 1878 and established his business, Hicks Ice Cream Company, in a large, modern building at 1216 State Street, just down the road from Presque Isle Bay. "He housed his ice cream 'factory' in the basement, an ice cream parlor on the first floor and an apartment on the second floor, which he shared with his wife Frances and daughter Ida." Even the concrete sidewalk in front of his business was modern, believed to be the first of its kind on State Street.

A clipping from the 1888 *City of Erie, PA*, shared by the Hagen History Center, reads, "Mr. Hicks has been engaged in the confectionary and ice-cream business for many years and his name has become a synonym for square dealing. His ice-cream plant at 1216 State street is one of the most complete in Western Pennsylvania, having a capacity of freezing 20 gallons of ice cream per hour, which can readily be increased by 40 gallons."

Hicks quickly became known for his delicious ice cream, and he prided himself on using high-quality ingredients. According to Sherry's story,

PURE ICE CREAM,

Manufactured for the
Wholesale
and
Retail Trade.

Furnished in any
Quantities
at Short Notice.

The Largest Manufacturer of
ICE CREAM AND ICES of any
concern in Pennsylvania outside of
Philadelphia.

**A Trial Order
Solicited.**

If you get it of Hicks you will find it to be Good.

All Orders by Mail or Telephone Given Prompt Attention.

J. S. HICKS,   -   1218 State Street.

JOHN S. HICKS, Erie's Leading Confectioner and
Ice Cream Manufacturer.

Above: Hicks Ice Cream Company advertisement. *Hagen History Center*.

Left: John S. Hicks, owner of Hicks Ice Cream Company, published in the 1898 *Erie Daily Times*. *Hagen History Center*.

advertisements from the time for the Hicks Ice Cream Company show that his ice cream was enjoyed at picnics, parties and church socials. It was very likely enjoyed often near the lakeshore as well, helping residents stay cool in the hot summer sun.

In 1905, he was granted a U.S. patent for a mold that could hold up to a pint of ice cream. He was quoted as saying, "My invention is an improved ice-cream mold for molding a brick of ice-cream with a figure of any desired form in the center thereof."

According to Sherry, his other shop specialties included water ices, Roman punches (which often were topped with a floating meringue) and Charlotte Russe, which was a combination of cake and frozen custard. Hicks was quite inventive at his company, which was one of the largest and most successful ice cream makers and distributors in the state, and he was the first to use electricity to freeze his ice cream. He was even chosen by the governor of Pennsylvania in 1915 to be a delegate to the Illinois National Half-Century Exposition, in Chicago, to celebrate the fiftieth anniversary of the Emancipation Proclamation.

Hicks died in 1933, after a long and successful career, and is buried at the Erie Cemetery. The "Hicks Block," with the words *Ice Cream* visible just under the roofline, stood on State Street until the early 1970s when it was torn down.

In S.B. Nelson's 1896 published book, *Nelson's Biographical Dictionary and Historical Reference Book of Erie County*, he called Hicks "one of the most prosperous and influential men of African descent that ever lived in Erie."

McGARVEY'S BOAT DRIVE-IN RESTAURANT

Sometimes the best restaurants aren't the fanciest ones, but rather the ones that make you feel at home no matter how you're dressed. For many visitors in Vermilion, that restaurant was McGarvey's Boat Drive-In. A vintage McGarvey's postcard states, "Informal Atmosphere—Come as U R."

"The riverside restaurant had its humble beginnings in the early years of the 20th century as a very lucrative bait and livery shop owned by a family named Showalter," wrote Rich Tarrant on VermilionOhio.org. "Originally the seasonal operation was located on the east bank of the Vermilion River just south of the current bridge."

In 1925, a Lorain couple by the name of Helfrich bought the property and built a restaurant, specializing in serving fish, chicken, steak and frogs' leg dinners.

Top: Bridge across Vermilion River, 1949. *Author's collection.*

Bottom: McGarvey's Restaurant. *Author's collection.*

In 1929, when the new (current) bridge was constructed over the river, and the old one was demolished, the Helfriches built a new summer and winter restaurant and boathouse just north of the bridge. Home-cooked dinners, fish, chicken, sandwiches (including hot fish sandwiches on Schwensen's bread, which was a revolutionary menu item at the time) and homemade pie were featured on the menu.

According to DiscoverVermilion.com, Helfrich's became a busy place, and the canoe and boat business also thrived. The restaurant changed hands several times until a man named Charles "Charlie" McGarvey, who had a restaurant named McGarvey's in Sandusky, bought it in 1938. One year later, the restaurant's name changed from Helfrich's to McGarvey's, and the bait and livery shop was closed.

An old ad boasts: "The only boat drive-in restaurant on the Great Lakes invites you to join the many who have found out how delicious food can be!"

A 1930s McGarvey's menu, on VintageMenuArt.com, shows that a filet mignon steak sandwich was considered the "house specialty" and was only $0.95. A "Super duper steak burger" was $0.55, fresh perch was $0.45 and a "golden brown shrimp plate" was $1.25. Pie "baked fresh daily" or "mom's old-fashioned cheesecake" was $0.30 per slice!

After McGarvey's death in the 1940s, the restaurant was bought and run by the Solomon family, who decided to keep the McGarvey name, and the restaurant continued to grow.

According to Cris Glaser from the *Morning Journal*, at the height of its popularity, following a 1970s expansion from two hundred to four hundred seats, McGarvey's was bringing in $2.5 million in sales per year and employed more than one hundred restaurant staff.

The restaurant began incorporating innovative changes that drew in new crowds. It made a smaller, kid's version of the restaurant's popular broiled tenderloin tip dinner, it deboned fresh Lake Erie pickerel in front of customers at the table and it encouraged children to pick a toy from its "treasure chest," like a plastic bracelet or toy car.

"At a typical Friday evening seafood buffet with the perch individually breaded in the kitchen, the restaurant pulled in $20,000 in sales receipts and a waitress could pocket $150 in tips for the night," said Eddie Solomon in Glaser's article. "You could come in a mink coat or Bermuda shorts. You still felt like you were part of the family."

It was one of the most well-known restaurants along the lakeshore, among both "landlubbers" and boaters alike. Alongside an order of steak, the restaurant's whipped mashed potatoes were one of its most popular side dishes.

The back of an old postcard reads, "Many outstanding features: Sip Sup N Sail (Enjoy a cocktail, dinner, and a boat ride). Award winning Kiddies Menu—King Sized Cocktails with free sauerkraut balls—entertainment."

Inside McGarvey's Boat Drive-In Restaurant, 1970s. *Author's collection.*

For nearly three-quarters of a century, the restaurant at McGarvey's Landing was a popular meeting place. Then, in 1990, the Solomons retired and sold the restaurant. It changed hands several times until 2000, when the Vermilion Port Authority bought the property and razed the building. It became a transient marina and restaurant named Red Clay on the River, now Quaker, Steak and Lube.

CAPTAIN FRANK'S LOBSTER HOUSE

A trip to Captain Frank's Lobster House practically felt like being in a boat on Lake Erie, with all the sights, smells and sounds. The hot, humid days and vibrant sunsets kept visitors lounging near the water late into the evening.

The restaurant was on the East Ninth Street Pier, which according to a postcard from the time was adjacent to the "Downtown Airport" (Burke Lakefront) and "only 300 feet from ballgames at Cleveland Stadium" (now Cleveland Browns Stadium). The back of the postcard reads, "While waiting for the finest and most delightful dinner on Lake Erie's shores, Capt. Frank invites you for a ride on his yacht. Varied menu includes fish, fresh caught from Capt. Frank's Boats."

The restaurant brings back a multitude of memories. According to Chris Roy's article on the Cleveland Historical website, "Some remember the place as 'wonderful' with the 'best seafood.' Others describe it as 'filthy,' 'dimly lit,' and 'a little creepy.'"

In 2018, when Cleveland.com asked which restaurant Clevelander's missed the most, Captain Frank's Lobster House topped the list. But it wasn't always called that. Sometimes the sign changed on a whim to Captain Frank's "Sea Food House," or sometimes both signs stood out front; regardless of its name, visitors kept coming back.

"Patrons could enjoy the sounds of a nearby Cleveland Indians baseball game or watch planes take off and land at Burke Lakefront Airport," wrote Roy. "Or perhaps they'd watch a romantic sunset; converse with fishermen; absorb Lake Erie's dubious smells; or fend off panhandlers, including one guy who lived outside the restaurant and called himself 'Captain Frank.'"

The real Captain Frank was Frank Visconti, who after emigrating from Sicily in 1914 sold fish from a horse-drawn buggy and operated the old Fulton Fish Market on East Twenty-Second Street and Woodland Avenue. Roy wrote that Captain Frank's Lobster House got its start in 1953 when

Captain Frank's Seafood/Lobster House on the East Ninth Street Pier. *Author's collection.*

Captain Frank with donkey and wagon imported from Palermo, Italy. *Author's collection.*

Visconti bought an abandoned boat depot on the pier and turned it into the beloved restaurant.

He brought his traditions from Italy to his new business, selling wine from Portofino and, according to a postcard, importing a donkey and wagon from Palermo, Italy, where they were used to transport wine from village to village. The postcard shows him pouring glasses of wine to beautiful women, dressed in traditional Sicilian fashion, sitting in the donkey-drawn cart.

The restaurant suffered a fire in 1958, but Visconti reopened a year later. "It flourished in the 1960s and 1970s, with great lake views, an indoor waterfall, festoons of fishing nets and frequently dirty lobster tanks providing all the ambiance families and couples could want," wrote Roy. "Notables ranging from Nelson Eddy, Judy Garland and Flip Wilson to Mott the Hoople and the Shah of Iran partied into the wee hours (or until they were asked to leave)."

Suzanne Ristagno recalled being at the restaurant during its heyday. "I worked at Capt. Franks! Night shift, good money! I always expected Tom Waits to walk in at 2:30 a.m. some crazy late night."

Even the drummer from the rock band The Who had a memorable visit to the restaurant, according to Tom Vavrek, who read the story in the book *Cleveland Rock and Roll Memories*, by Carlo Wolff. Mike Belkin, legendary Cleveland concert promoter, recalled this memory in the book:

> One time in Cleveland, after the Who had finished a date, we were all meeting down at Captain Frank's for dinner, and it was a great show, sold out at Public Hall, and the whole band was there and a couple of guys from the James Gang and we don't know where Keith Moon's at. We look over to see Dale Peters, the bass player from the James Gang, walk in with Keith Moon. When he was playing that night, he was wearing all white. When he walked into the restaurant, he was wearing all wet black. He was inebriated and fell off the pier, which happened to be about ten feet to the water. Dale threw him a life preserver and pulled him [out]. If Dale hadn't been walking by, Keith would have never come around. Keith was happy, having fun, couldn't have cared less, he was soaking wet, sat down as if nothing had ever happened.

For Rita Ann Farone Gaebelein, both of Captain Frank's businesses, the restaurant and the fish market, held a special place in her heart. As moderator of the Facebook page "Cleveland Downtown: Past and Present," she commented that Captain Frank's was the first place she ever had lobster and her first drink when she turned twenty-one in 1967. "My grandmother lived on 22nd Street (early '50s) and many Fridays we'd walk to the fish market for fresh fish," she wrote. "It was fascinating to see all those fresh fish in coolers and barrels filled to the brim with fish all over the store floor. It certainly didn't smell great, but it was amazing nevertheless."

She said the area where the fish market was located was known as "Cleveland's Big Italy" and was filled with many different immigrants of varying nationalities, ethnic groups and religions. "I always felt extremely lucky to have been born there," Gaebelein said. "I learned at an early age how important diversity is. Many would have considered this to be a poor, blue-collar area, I always felt the 'richness' of the area went far beyond money and material things."

Felix Giles reminisced about his time at Captain Frank's on "Cleveland Downtown: Past and Present." He said the folks who worked there were always wonderful to him when he visited with his U.S. Navy uniform on. "Back in the early '70s, whenever I would come home on leave, they would always fix my favorite milkshake, strawberry and banana mix, and would never charge me!"

After Visconti died in 1984, the restaurant was sold, and the new owner declared bankruptcy five years later, amid growing competition. The building was demolished in 1994. Today, the pier looks much different. Visitors can play a game at the Cleveland Pier Volleyball Courts, watch a concert at Voinovich Bicentennial Park or take a boat tour aboard the *Goodtime III*.

LAKE ROAD INN

The legendary Lake Road Inn opened in Avon Lake in 1923, at Lake Shore Electric Stop 41, near the city's eastern end. "Only 16 miles from public square," boasts a 1930s ad. "A beautiful drive out Lake Road."

It was promoted as having the finest dance floor in northern Ohio, offering dancing every evening for up to five hundred people and seating for just as many guests in its dining room, where, according to a vintage ad, steak, duck, chicken, lobster and "frog dinners" were served.

Guy Lombardo and His Royal Canadian Orchestra were noted performers at the inn early in their careers, according to a blog about Lorain County's history and nostalgia by Dan Brady. They had just recorded their first album months before.

Then, in October 1926, the Inn was badly damaged in a fire. (It had been closed about six weeks earlier by the Lorain County sheriff due to alleged liquor law violations.) The origin of the blaze was unknown but was believed to be intentionally set, and it wasn't the only fire in the area under investigation.

According to an October 18, 1926 *Lorain Times-Herald* article shared on the blog, "Wednesday's fire adds another chapter to the series of mysterious blazes which have been reported along the Lake-Rd between Lorain and Cleveland during the last year."

THE CIRCLE INN

For several decades, the Circle Inn on Lakeshore Road was the place to go in Athol Springs, New York. Just west of Buffalo, it was said to offer the best view of the lake shoreline headed toward the city, before the new Lakeshore Road cut through the property.

According to Steve Cichon on BuffaloStories.com, the Strohm family owned the Circle Inn from 1939 to 1963, and the property was divided into twenty smaller lots for summer homes. At one point in 1950, the inn offered "the only lakefront properties available between Buffalo and Evans, only 9 miles from Lafayette Square."

It was across the street from Red Top Hot Dogs and not far from Hoak's, where an image of an ice-encased car went viral, making national news during a January 2016 winter storm. It became a "go-to" spot, according to Cichon, for TV news crews to broadcast from in the winter to show the wicked fury of Lake Erie wind and waves hitting the shore.

Although Frank Strohm was often seen behind the bar as the face of the inn, his wife, Mary, was the legal owner. The restaurant had many successful years and eventually became known as the Seacrest Supper Club after the Strohm family sold it. The building burned down in 1968.

FAIRPORT ICE PALACE

For a fleeting moment in the late 1890s, a glittering ice palace spiraled up into the sky along the shores of Lake Erie in Fairport, Ohio.

According to Saul C. Olin's book *The Story of Fairport, Ohio*, newspaper accounts from the time described it as a huge "ice palace" with beautiful pinnacles, sparkling turrets and huge doorways. It was advertised all over Ohio as an Ice Carnival, and a newspaper article said it was "studded with a thousand electric lights-rivaling Montreal's biggest carnival."

In the bitter cold of February, with winds whipping off the lake, 150 men worked on the castle structure for days. An elaborate program was planned for the ice castle's reveal, and people came from all over to see it. Anticipation was high. Then, on the last day, when the palace was nearly completed, the sun broke from behind the clouds, bright and strong overhead, causing the temperatures to quickly rise into the upper forties. This did not bode well for the palace.

"Towers, turrets, battlements and drawbridges toppled into the open waters," reads Olin's book. "All that remained was a yawning hole in the ice."

INDUSTRIES BEHIND BEACH GLASS

The beaches of Lake Erie lure visitors for different reasons—to cool off in the water, enjoy a vibrant sunset or stroll the beach, searching for treasures churned up by the waves. That includes unique rocks, fossils and beach glass (called "sea glass") along the ocean.

There's a thrill in finding these shining jewels in shallow water and half-buried in sand. Sometimes calm waters gently push marbles ashore, while larger pieces can be churned up by a storm.

According to my eldest son, Lake Erie "can be foggy, sunny or destructive," and like the weather that affects it, you only must wait a short time for conditions to change.

Collectors make jewelry out of beach glass or display it in jars, showcasing the rarity of the colors. Reds, purples and pinks are among the rarest, while white, pale blues, brown and green are most common. Some even consider it trash, and in fact it often was cast off by fishermen and industries in and around the lake. Each piece, often found near once-busy shipping ports or factories, is like a clue to our region's history.

Glass

In the 1800s, glass was hand-blown into molds, according to Richard LaMotte in *Pure Sea Glass*. "By the early 1900s, the birth of the automated glass bottle machine altered everything," wrote LaMotte. "Bottles were soon being produced in the millions in many U.S. glass houses." By the 1960s, the nation's glass industry was declining as unbreakable metal and plastic containers were more sought after in American homes.

Close-up view of vitrite slag. *Emily Mann.*

Its color is generally the best clue in identifying its age and source. "Most rugged looking 'black glass' dates prior to the mid-1800s, while smoother forms could be remnants of latter-day Depression glass," according to LaMotte. "Yellow-green 'Vaseline glass' could date prior to 1930, and ribbed, soft green pieces common to Coca-Cola bottles hail from 1915 to roughly 1970."

One of the most challenging types of glass to identify and date is slag from glass factories. "This is commonly referred to as 'end-of-day' slag and can sometimes be found with mixed colors if one color was being added to flush out an existing color from molten pots or processing equipment," wrote LaMotte in *The Lure of Sea Glass.*

Emily Mann of Sandusky found more than one hundred pieces of vitrite slag at Harrington Point Beach in Conneaut, Ohio, in 2020. Vitrite was used as an electric insulator and found in the base of common incandescent lightbulbs, like the ones produced at the now defunct General Electric (GE) plant in Conneaut.

According to an article in *Sea Glass Journal,* it's mainly made of ground glass with lead oxide and manganese oxide, creating its dark-purple color. GE glass is deep cobalt blue or black amethyst, which people often pass up because it can look like a rock. The best way to test "black glass" is to hold it up to see if light passes through it.

The GE plant operated from 1941 to 2008, and it's rumored that in the 1950s and '60s the company dumped its discarded glass along the shoreline as landfill to combat erosion.

Emily Mann also finds glass on the beaches of Lion's Park in Sandusky that she believes may be left over from Enterprise Glass Works, which briefly existed down the road in the early 1900s.

According to a blog on Sandusky history, it was once a booming industry on Superior Street, on the city's west side. A page in the 1905 Sanborn Fire Insurance Map shows how close the company was to Sandusky Bay. In the early years, the glass was hand-blown at Enterprise Glass Works and then flattened in another part of the plant. At the end of each day, employees were said to use leftover glass to make canes and other unique items. In 1910, one hundred men were employed by the company, but by 1916, it was in receivership; by the 1920s, the Sandusky Glass Manufacturing and Supply Company was operating in its place.

Locals believe that the glass could also come from wineries and breweries that existed along the shoreline.

Marbles

One of the most exciting beach glass finds are marbles, with their swirling colors and unique designs. My kids and I have been lucky enough to find a few, but we always wonder where they came from.

One longtime, often-debated theory is that ships traveling on Lake Erie used marbles as ballast to provide stability. Experts say that if they did use marbles, they were likely clay, which was most commonly manufactured. According to the Marble Collectors Society of America, many were produced in Germany and used as ballast in the keels of ships that sailed to America and then were removed and sold. Considering the large number of shipwrecks, it's possible that some went down with the ship and ended up on the shorelines. (Other sources say marbles would never have been used as ballast and that items that could be sold upon arrival at ports would have been more cost effective.)

Marble found by author's son on shores of Lake Erie. *Photo by author.*

Clay marbles were also made at the American Marble & Toy Manufacturing Company in Akron, Ohio, the first toy marble factory in the United States. According to the American Toy Marble Museum's website, in the mid-1890s it mass-produced 1 million marbles and dozens of "penny toys" each day. (Author note: You can learn more about this by watching a documentary I wrote and co-produced with Larry Baker that aired on PBS called *The Original North Pole*.)

Museum director Michael Cahill believes that marbles found in the lake are due to the popularity the tiny toy once had, especially in the 1930s. He said that in 1938, more than 25 million children competed in marble tournaments, and one of the largest was the Greater Cleveland District Marbles Tournament, held at Edge Water Park from 1923 to 1951. Marbles from the tournament may have made their way into Lake Erie.

Also, many children began playing with marbles when they were very young, and by the time they were teenagers, they had acquired a large collection that they then used as slingshot ammo to shoot out into the lake or at targets, like rats, at local dumps.

Bricks

For many years, it was commonplace for municipalities to dump their garbage in rivers or streams, and many lakeside cities towed their garbage out on a barge to dump into Lake Erie. They also discarded old bricks into the lake, including street pavers that can be more than a century old. You can still see the names of the brickmakers on the sides of many, like Alliance Clay, Buckeye and Besser Youngstown.

According to a 2019 *Cleveland Plain Dealer* article, Chad Waffen, a scuba diver with a degree in archaeology, has noticed bricks made of marble washing up in Lakewood. "I have to assume the marble bricks are the result of an early 1900s skyscraper or other building that was demolished and

Buckeye brick lying on Lake Erie beach. *Photo by author.*

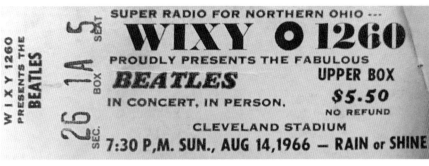

Top: Cleveland Stadium being built, April 6, 1931. *Photo by Gus A. Fretter, Library of Congress.*

Bottom: Ticket to the Beatles concert, Municipal (Cleveland) Stadium, August 14, 1966. *Mary Joanne (Perusek) Boresz.*

dumped and are washing in as they are all over the lake bottom leading into the beach. They just don't make bricks like that anymore."

In fact, the old Cleveland Municipal Stadium is now underwater and may be contributing to the bricks that wash ashore. The stadium stood in downtown Cleveland from 1931 through 1996. According to a Case Western Reserve University (CWRU) article about Cleveland Municipal Stadium, at the time it was built it had the largest individual seating capacity of any outdoor arena in the world, capable of fitting more than seventy-eight thousand fans. The Cleveland Indians played their first game there in 1932.

It hosted the World Series in 1948 and 1954, and the Beatles held a concert at the stadium on August 14, 1966. My mom, Mary Joanne (Perusek) Boresz, remembers the excitement of being in the crowd. "The Beatles ran onto the field to a thunderous ovation....I had never heard anything like that before in my life. We could barely see the Beatles because of the distance, they looked like miniatures of themselves. It didn't matter though, we could see well enough and we knew that down on that field that John, Paul and George were busy strumming their guitars while Ringo pounded away on the drums."

Then the Cleveland Browns football team played there for many years until they left the city, and the only hope of bringing another team in involved demolishing the stadium and building a new one.

According to Case Western Reserve University, wrecking balls began clearing away portions of the bleachers in November 1996, along with the Donald Gray Gardens, which had been built behind the stadium in 1936 for the Great Lakes Exposition. A quarter of the old concrete stadium was eventually relocated a half mile offshore to create fishing reefs—about six hundred feet long, twenty to fifty feet wide and two to fifteen feet high. One is offshore Euclid General Hospital; another is off Perkins Beach, just west of Edgewater Park. According to Rockthelake.com, a third is located near Bratenahl. One section is said to have a row of seats still left intact.

According to Geoffrey Reutter, former director of Ohio Sea Grant, which helped develop the reefs, ten reefs were sunk between 1984 and 2000 between Lorain and Euclid. The reefs attract up to sixty-six times as many fish as the surrounding area, which means more anglers come to fish and spend money at nearby businesses.

AMUSEMENT PARKS

EUCLID BEACH AMUSEMENT PARK

Many people were moving from rural areas to big cities as business was booming during the Industrial Revolution of the 1800s. They had more disposable income and free time, so entrepreneurs began building amusement parks along the lakeshore to accommodate them on acres of land that used to be picnic groves or farmland.

"Some amusement parks, first known as trolley parks, were started by streetcar companies, usually at the end of a line to generate weekend business," according to *Euclid Beach Park*, written by Euclid Beach Park Now.

The Cleveland area had minor parks operating in the 1890s, but none stood out quite like Euclid Beach Amusement Park. It opened on June 22, 1895, on about sixty-three acres of land in Euclid Township (later Cleveland). The main entrance, marked by an iconic arch, was on Lake Shore Boulevard, near East 156th Street. "The original Arch was constructed of wood. By the late 1920s, it was decided to cover it with permastone, a product that looks very much like real stone," according to *Euclid Beach Park*.

My mom, Mary Joanne (Perusek) Boresz, grew up in Euclid and has happy memories of taking a bus to Euclid Beach Park with her parents, John and Margaret Perusek, and sister, Peggy (Landig) Zirbes, in the 1950s and '60s.

She remembers rushing off the bus and passing the kiddie rides as they made their way into the park. The memories are as vivid now as the

Arch entrance to Euclid Beach Park, circa 1945. *Author's collection.*

John, Peggy, Mary Joanne and Margaret Perusek, 1963. *Mary Joanne (Perusek) Boresz.*

Bathing pavilion and pier, Euclid Beach Park on Lake Erie's shore. *Author's collection.*

experience was back then. "I heard the roar of the coasters as we walked down the entranceway and felt the vibration of the rides as they rumbled like thunder in the near distance," my mom recalled. "As we entered the park and I looked around, I could see that people were everywhere. Some walked slowly, glancing skyward as they decided which ride would be their next, while others ran to get in line for their choice of seats. Kids laughed and squealed, running from ride to ride."

Some of the park's earliest structures included an eighteen-thousand-square-foot dance pavilion, a bathhouse with an upper-level restaurant, the Avenue Theater and a wooden pier, welcoming people who arrived by steamship, while others arrived via trolley.

"It was originally divided down the center by a wooden railing to separate arriving and departing steamer passengers," reads *Euclid Beach Park*. "During the first five years of operation, the canopied area at the end of the Pier is where the majority of visitors arrived onboard one of the two steamers, also known as 'Tubs,' owned by the Euclid Beach Park Company. The *Duluth* and the *Superior* steamers were painted white with bright red letters and could each carry 800 passengers from downtown Cleveland."

By 1897, new attractions included a Ferris wheel, a walk-through fun house called the Crystal Maze, a switchback railway and a merry-go-round.

The Humphrey family, who ran successful popcorn stands in Cleveland, became synonymous with Euclid Beach at this time when they opened their first stand in the park. However, they felt that some aspects of the park were unsavory, like the beer garden, sideshows and gambling. According to *Euclid Beach Park*, park management refused to remove them, so the Humphreys decided not to renew their lease.

In 1900, financial challenges forced Euclid Beach Park owners to close. However, the Humphreys saw great potential, if only they could do things their way, and offered to lease the park from the owners. The new Euclid Beach, founded on higher morals, reopened a year later. "Under their ownership and management, the lakefront amusement park was operated on the foundation of fair dealing, clean entertainment, and pleasant surroundings," reads *Euclid Beach Park*.

The new family atmosphere was a success. In place of beer, visitors enjoyed Phez Loganberry Juice, which outsold Hire's Root Beer and Vernor's Ginger Ale. The only drawback was that it fermented into alcohol if it wasn't refrigerated, which put an end to the popular juice.

The park also became known for its Humphrey's popcorn balls and saltwater taffy, still sold at locations around Cleveland. (According to my dad, Dale Boresz, Mr. Humphrey was a frequent customer at Cleveland Trust Bank, in downtown Cleveland, where my grandpa Will Boresz worked as safe deposit manager, and he sometimes gave my grandpa these sought-after confections to take home to my grandma June Boresz and their six children. He often wrote on the bag, "For June, Will, and the six D's.")

The pier, Euclid Beach Park. *Author's collection.*

Will and June Boresz and their "six D's"—Dale, Diane, David, Doreen, Debbie and Donna, circa 1960s. *Mary Joanne and Dale Boresz.*

A big event occurred at the park in late August 1910 when Glenn H. Curtiss, aviator and founder of the U.S. aircraft industry, took off from the beach in a biplane and flew to Cedar Point in Sandusky. According to *Euclid Beach Park*, at the time it was the longest flight over water.

The Humphreys added new rides and attractions each year. Between 1901 and 1910, that included the Velvet Coaster (later the Aero Dips), Figure 8 Coaster, Aerial Swing, Scenic Railway, Flying Ponies and the grand four-row Carousel. The Derby Racer (the Racing Coaster) remained a fixture at Euclid Beach for decades.

"A Sea Swing, in the 1920s, occupied the circular pool just west of the Bath House on the beach next to the Pier," reads *Euclid Beach Park*. "A sort of water ride, with a merry-go-round configuration but without horses, it whisked riders in strap-like seats just above the water's surface. The rotation was powered electrically. The Fountain was placed in this area once the ride was dismantled."

A rectangular pool east of the bathhouse was also popular but had strict regulations on bathing garments, requiring them to cover limbs and chest with no gaudy colors.

Big changes took place in the 1920s and '30s, including the addition of two signature coasters: the Thriller and Flying Turns, along with the Dippy Whip, Flying Scooters, Sleepy Hollow Railroad, the Great American Racing Derby, Dodgems, Kiddie Land and the Bug, which was my mom's first choice to ride at the park.

"I loved it and could ride on it all day long," she told me. "The Bug was green if I recall and looked just like a bug to me. It had single round cars that could hold several people at a time seated in a circle. The cars were in a line, one behind the other and swung rapidly around the track in a circular motion, taking corners so fast that riders squealed in delight as they bumped back and forth into each other."

The Surprise House with Laughing Sam and Laughing Sal was another addition that decade, which became a beloved, and often feared, part of the park. "As we walked through the ride area, we always passed Laughing Sal, a big laughing mannequin that stood outside the Fun House," recalled my mom. "She was huge with a loud hysterical laugh. Sal had a monstrous smile, was larger than life and jiggled from side to side nonstop. I liked the tilted floor inside and the silly mirrors that made us laugh. The little air holes in the floor that sprayed air when you stepped on them was too much

Above: Rocket Ships, Euclid Beach Park. *Author's collection.*

Opposite: Ticket to the Milkmen's Picnic at Euclid Beach Park, June 20, 1945. *Author's collection.*

for me, and Grandpa always had to take me out through an emergency exit before we had finished. Often, I was near tears begging to leave the Fun House."

Another favorite ride was the tunnel ride, Laugh in the Dark, which was filled with surprises: "I don't remember much of what I saw on that ride except at the end of it the dark room suddenly filled with bright stars spinning around me. It made me feel dizzy to watch it but fascinating too. I felt like I was on a rocket ship to the moon and was flying though outer space!"

She remembers going from ride to ride with my Grandma and Grandpa Perusek and Aunt Peggy throughout the day until they were exhausted. Before heading home, they often rode on the Rocket Ships near the lake (which began as the Aerial Swing, with wicker gondolas, later replaced by airplanes and then stainless steel rocket ships, built by the park's maintenance staff).

"The ride was nestled among tall trees, and the ships would glide by them smoothly," my mom recalled. "There was often a gentle wind blowing in from the lake that created a calming effect as the ships gracefully swept along the trees. As we rode along, I would look out at the lake and imagine we were flying over it."

During the Great Depression, Euclid Beach was a welcome respite because there was no entry fee, and rides and food purchases were bought with tickets. Then, in the time after World War II, interest in the turn-of-the-century amusement parks declined, and many closed. In an effort to draw in a new generation, Euclid Beach introduced new attractions in the '50s and '60s, like the Rotor, Giant Slide and Antique Cars, and began hosting rock-and-roll concerts with bands like Lovin' Spoonful, Gary Lewis and the Playboys and the Beach Boys.

Flying Turns, Euclid Beach Park. *Author's collection.*

According to *Euclid Beach Park*, the Beach Boys paid tribute to Euclid Beach in their recording "Amusement Parks U.S.A" with the line, "At Euclid Beach Park on the Flying Turns, I bet you can't keep from smilin'."

"Though Euclid Beach was a place of fun and excitement during the day, when the sun set over Lake Erie and the lights came on throughout the park, it became a land of enchantment," reads *Euclid Beach Park*.

Fifteen minutes before the park's nightly closing, the manager rode his bike from his office to the Thriller. "The lights on top of the Thriller lift hill could be seen from most of the park," according to the book. "A few minutes before closing each ride, someone stood at each electric breaker box. When the manager gave his signal, the Thriller went dark, and within 5 to 10 seconds all the rides were dark."

Although Euclid Beach was still a beloved place to visit, competition increased from nearby Cedar Point and Geauga Lake amusement parks, and by the end of the 1968 season, the Humphreys had announced that the park would close the following year, on September 28, 1969.

Many remember that devastating day, including my father-in-law, Dave Engelking, who visited the park with friends a few weeks after it closed. They mischievously wandered around the empty park, saying one last goodbye to some of their favorite rides like the Funhouse, the Thriller and Flying Turns, and he couldn't resist grabbing a star up on the wall of the tunnel in the Laugh in the Dark. (However, that star is long gone...lost to time.)

After Euclid Beach closed, the property was sold to developers. High-rise senior apartments and a nursing home were built, and part of the property became Cleveland Metroparks' Euclid Beach Park. Some remnants remain, including pieces of the pier, an outline of the fountain and the Rocket Ships, which have been motorized to carry people around at private events throughout Northeast Ohio.

The famous Euclid Beach arch, designated a historic Cleveland landmark, still stands today. Some of the rides, including the Great American Racing Derby, were moved to Cedar Point, where it operates as Cedar Downs. The Euclid Beach Park Grand Carousel can be found at the Cleveland History Center, allowing those who once rode it at Euclid Beach to take another spin down memory lane.

My mom remembers the magic of riding the carousel as a child:

I held on to the reins and pretended I was guiding my pony to our magic castle. The music started, and the horses gracefully moved along, faster and faster. As the carousel turned, the ponies moved up and down. I could feel the wind through my hair as we galloped along. The lake breeze cooling me off as we spun around. Much too soon, the ride ended.

A sentiment felt by many who miss the joy and exhilaration of a day spent at Euclid Beach.

LAKE ERIE PARK AND CASINO

Lake Erie Park and Casino, in Toledo, was a byproduct of the early twentieth century's explosion of industrial wealth, offering workers and their families an escape from the smoke-filled city.

Opening in 1895, it offered guests gambling, live music performances and a variety of amusement park–style rides and entertainments (spanning part of what is now Bay View Park and the Detwiler Park Golf Course).

"A landscaped 'midway' promenade led patrons past a merry-go-round, hall of mirrors and miniature railway ride, among a rotating cast of attractions on approach to the boardwalk," according to Stefan Binion on MidStory.org. "A streetcar line running along Summit Street connected Point Place (a separate municipality until 1937) with downtown Toledo in minutes, and the casino entrance formed the line's terminus."

Boardwalk, casino, portion of scenic railway at Lake Erie Park and Casino in Toledo, Ohio, circa 1900–1910. *Library of Congress.*

Four years after the park opened, the boardwalk was engulfed in flames and destroyed. A cause was never determined. Another, even larger casino was quickly built, and just as it was nearly completed, it also caught on fire. The owners were determined and rebuilt. Yet again, it burned down. In 1902, in a fourth attempt, another casino was opened on the site and was grander than ever.

According to Binion, it sat on a lengthened boardwalk extending more than 1,200 feet into Lake Erie and included an auditorium with seating for up to 3,500 people. It was becoming a beloved summertime destination until Toledo Beach resort and amusement park opened across the state line in LaSalle, Michigan, in 1906.

"The rival resort was newer and located on a beach with sand; the casino boardwalk stretched over marsh and reeds before reaching clearer lake water. Even worse for Toledo Casino, Toledo Beach was both further from the city (and thus the pollution) and still easily accessible by trolley," reads MidStory.org.

To save it, the Toledo Railways and Light Company, which owned the streetcar line that serviced the casino and most other public places throughout the city, bought it in 1907. However, by 1910, the casino had burned a fourth and final time. The fire was said to spread so quickly that it turned the massive complex into ash in less than forty-five minutes. It was never rebuilt, and nothing remains of it except for a few artificial ponds that once lined the Lake Erie Park midway, which are now water feature obstacles in the Detwiler Park Golf Course.

TOLEDO BEACH AMUSEMENT PARK

With a name like Toledo Beach Amusement Park, you might assume that it was in Toledo, Ohio. However, it was just over the state line in LaSalle, Michigan.

According to David L. Eby in the *Monroe News*, the four-hundred-acre waterfront venue was called the Ottawa Beach Resort before the Toledo Rail Light and Power Company bought the resort, transforming it into Toledo Beach Amusement Park. "An electric trolley service brought visitors from Ohio to the park," wrote Eby. "Many had no idea they crossed over the state line into Michigan."

Interurban trolleys made stops along the way at locations like Lakeside and Luna Pier, when the park was at its peak in the early 1900s, and the accessibility of the interurbans helped turn the region into a resort.

One of the main features, Toledo Beach Dance Hall, was illuminated with electric lights powered by its own power plant. The unique, glittering nighttime view was a huge draw since the novelty of electricity was still very new.

There was also a three-hundred-room bathhouse, where guests could rent a bathing suit (made of wool and covering a good portion of their body) to swim for the day. A massive wooden water slide was built in the lake, but it was damaged by a bad storm in 1917.

Even a famous aviator from the Wright Brothers Flying School in Dayton visited. According to Eby, on June 26, 1913, Harry Atwood caused quite a frenzy among visitors, most of whom had never seen a plane fly before, when he landed his seaplane built by the Wright brothers.

Throughout the years, like Lake Erie Park and Casino, Toledo Beach suffered through storms and fires that damaged and destroyed buildings and rides. Yet the park drew visitors until the rise of the automobile gave people the flexibility to travel to bigger and better parks.

Toledo Beach slowly declined until the interurban trolleys stopped running in 1927. The park closed during the Depression but reopened

"Electric effect" of the Toledo Beach dance hall at night, 1908. *Author's collection.*

Toledo Beach, 1909. *Author's collection.*

Water Toboggan, Toledo Beach, 1916. *Author's collection.*

and closed again several times through the 1950s. After closing for good, the area was dredged and converted into a marina, known today as Safe Harbor Toledo Beach.

ERIE BEACH AMUSEMENT PARK

Dancers filled the floor of the Erie Beach Amusement Park casino on a midsummer evening. The only respite from the stifling heat was an occasional cool breeze coming off Lake Erie.

The three-story casino was the focal building of the park, which was located along the Canadian shores of Lake Erie, across the Niagara River from downtown Buffalo and southwest of the Peace Bridge (connecting the United States and Canada, at the eastern edge of Lake Erie).

According to the *Fort Erie Post*, "On the lake side of the Casino, was a concrete swimming pool which was billed as The World's Largest Swimming Pool. It had a sand covered bottom, sloped from three to eight to nine feet in depth. Lake water was continuously pumped into it so the water was completely replaced every 24 hours. A similar children's pool was created on the east side of the Casino."

The casino had dressing and washing rooms, a dance floor with a hanging platform for the orchestra and a restaurant, with the Erie Beach Hotel right behind it.

The park got its start in the 1800s as Snake Hill Grove, a wooded picnic area along the lakeshore. According to the website 1,000 Towns of Canada, the park catered primarily to Buffalo residents. Then, in 1904, the land was bought, and plans were soon underway to build an amusement park.

Before 1927 and the opening of the Peace Bridge, visitors often arrived by ferry from Black Rock, New York, to Fort Erie South, Ontario, aboard large steamers from downtown Buffalo or by car for Canadians.

Once inside the park, guests could stroll down a one-thousand-foot-long lakefront promenade, stopping at various midway concessions. There were roller coaster rides and two small stadiums featuring circus acts, along with equestrian shows and the casino, known for years later as "the old dance hall."

According to *Fort Erie Post*, "it was promoted as the best dance hall around. It was a place for music, dancing and of course gambling. Wealthy Americans were most welcome and they came both rich and poorer. The Dance Hall became the central meeting place."

Top: "The World's Largest Swimming Pool," Erie Beach Amusement Park, circa late 1800s/ early 1900s. *Niagara Falls (Ontario) Public Library.*

Bottom: Swimmers and parkgoers in front of three-story Casino, Erie Beach Amusement Park, circa late 1800s/early 1900s. *Niagara Falls (Ontario) Public Library.*

Like with other parks, the rise of automobiles caused a decline in the guests at Erie Beach, and in the 1920s, parkgoers were able to drive to Crystal Beach Amusement Park, a few miles to the west.

Erie Beach Amusement Park's final season was in 1930, when it went bankrupt and closed. Many of the rides were torn down or sold to other parks. The hotel burned down in 1935, and the casino sat abandoned until the late 1970s, when it was demolished.

According to the Western New York Heritage website, part of the concrete swimming pool wall and pump house are now landmarks along the lakeshore at Waverly Beach Park. Remnants of the old pier, light posts and outdoor pavilion are slowly being overtaken by nature. A concrete promenade was built in 2008 for visitors to walk among the ruins, imagining the grandeur and excitement that once existed there.

CRYSTAL BEACH AMUSEMENT PARK, ONTARIO

In the middle of the Roaring Twenties, flappers danced the fast-paced Charleston across the crowded floor of the massive Crystal Ballroom at Crystal Beach Amusement Park in Ontario. It opened in 1925 and could hold up to three thousand people, making it the largest dance hall in North America at the time.

The park opened in the late 1800s, and although it was located in Canada, it was known as Buffalo's Coney Island. Until the Peace Bridge opened, visitors from America arrived by boat, like the *Americana*, a passenger excursion steamer that brought thousands of visitors a day from downtown Buffalo for decades.

Another majestic steamer, *Canadiana*, made its maiden voyage from Buffalo to Crystal Beach a few years later. "It was a luxurious boat designed in a Victorian style," according to Brock University Library's Archives and Special Collections. "There were stained glass windows, chandeliers, mahogany cabins, and grand staircases. In the large ballroom, there was entertainment which included: Cab Calloway, Woody Herman and Duke Ellington. There were even slot machines onboard until the Buffalo Police shut them down in the 1950s. Her last run to Crystal Beach was in 1956."

As attendance grew at the park, rides were added. Tim Sykes wrote on WayBackTimes.com that the earliest coasters included a Figure 8 and larger Backety-Bak switchback scenic railway and the bright-yellow Giant, built in 1916, which ran for seventy years.

"In 1927, Crystal Beach Park hired Harry Traver to design and build The Cyclone, still considered to be the most terrifying roller coaster ever built," wrote Sykes. "This magnificent thrill ride had an unorthodox track layout, which twisted and turned at steep angles throughout the entire ride, torturing its riders. The only straight section of track was the lift hill and the

Americana, 1909. *Author's collection.*

break run at the end of the ride." According to LakeGeorge.com, it was so extreme that a nurse's station was installed near the ride's exit.

Its design made it a maintenance and insurance headache, so after twenty years of thrills, the Cyclone was removed and replaced with the Comet in 1947, a four-thousand-foot-long coaster with a ninety-five-foot-tall lift hill that stood on a concrete base towering over Lake Erie's shoreline.

Yet according to memories posted on ExploringNiagara.com, the rides aren't the only thing that make parkgoers reminisce:

> *The two items of food that I can remember as being unique to Crystal Beach were the Sugar Waffles and the candy suckers. You could not leave the park without experiencing either. The candy suckers would be purchased and saved for the end of the day…making the ride home seem less painful, and no doubt giving our parents some much needed peace and quiet.*

According to Sykes, food concession buildings throughout the park sold popcorn, hot dogs and drinks, including a local loganberry beverage.

Sadly, after 101 summers, Crystal Beach Park closed following the 1989 season. Pieces were auctioned off, and several rides were purchased by other parks; the Comet moved to Six Flags Great Escape in Lake George, New York.

Crystal Beach (Ontario) scenic railway ride, 1909. *Author's collection.*

The Cyclone roller coaster, Crystal Beach (Ontario), 1930s. *Author's collection.*

The Crystal Beach miniature train ride is said to still entertain passengers on winery tours in Jordan, Ontario, and according to Sykes, "The Crystal Beach Logenberry beverage can be purchased at several stores in the Buffalo area. At various large outdoor events each summer, a local entrepreneur often sets up his concession, selling the famous Crystal Beach Sugar Waffles that are still hand made using the same equipment once used at the park. Yes, these are minor concessions, but tiny bits of Crystal Beach Park do live on."

Today, the lakefront homes of the Crystal Beach Tennis and Yacht Club span much of the land where the amusement park used to sit.

CRYSTAL BEACH PARK, VERMILION

On the other end, and opposite shore, of Lake Erie, another Crystal Beach was entertaining parkgoers in Vermilion, Ohio.

It began around 1870, according to the Vermilion Historical Society, as a picnic grove named Shadduck Lake Park. Pioneer farmer George Shadduck decided to transform his farm "from cow pasture into a picturesque public picnic grove and bathing beach," according to Rich Tarrant on VermilionOhio.org.

Tarrant noted that the amusement park opened in 1907 and quickly evolved. "Energized by widespread approval of this basic recreation facility he soon added a beer garden, gaming devices, and a dance hall. Thirty-two years later an area businessman, George H. Blanchat purchased the property with the intention of stepping things up a notch (or two or three)."

According to DiscoverVermilion.org, several historical plaques sit at the north end of Vermilion's Nantucket Place, depicting its history. One explains that the founders of Crystal Beach, George and Josephine Blanchat, purchased the 42.5 acres property in 1906, transforming half the land, along the lake, into an amusement park and the other half into the parking lot.

One plaque reads, "The name of the park is attributed to Josephine Blanchat. This occurred when on a walk along the beach with her husband she had picked up a handful of sand and remarked, 'It looks like crystal.'"

Soon, the park not only had a dancing pavilion, dining hall, carousel and shooting gallery but also many other concessions and rides. Some of the most popular included the Ferris wheel, Dodgem, Tumble-Bug, Loop-o-Plane, Left in the Dark, Rocket Ships and Thriller.

Crystal Beach Dancing Pavilion, Vermilion, 1920s. *Author's collection.*

The "rust removing crew," including the park manager, were brave souls who used a car and two oil cans to remove rust that built up over the winter months along the gravity-powered Thriller.

Its lakefront location was incorporated into one of the rides with a water toboggan that ran down a cliff into Lake Erie.

During the big band era, famous performers played in the ballroom, including Louis Armstrong, Sammy Kaye, Les Brown with Doris Day and the Everly Brothers, which according to the Vermilion Historical Society drew people from Cleveland, Toledo and Columbus.

Visitors arrived at Crystal Beach on the Lake Shore Electric interurban trolley (and then walked about a mile to the park), by car and by boat.

According to Tarrant, "On the night of April 20, 1947, tragedy struck. Fire claimed the two-story pavilion house, the roller-skating rink, penny arcade, refreshment stand, and several other rides located at the back, or northern part, of the park. But by July 4th of the same year a new single-story building housing the arcade and refreshment stand was built to replace the one lost in the fire."

The park remained in the Blanchat family, passed down through multiple generations, until it was sold in 1962. Today, the lakefront Crystal Shores Apartments stand where roller coasters once soared up into the sky.

EXPOSITIONS

W orld fairs and expositions were held in the late 1800s and early 1900s in major cities throughout Europe and America, including three bordering Lake Erie: Detroit, Cleveland and Buffalo. They were created to display the wonders of the Industrial Revolution and merge Western civilization with other global cultures. At first, the expos only focused on displays of technology and innovation, but they eventually added commercialized entertainment.

DETROIT INTERNATIONAL EXPOSITION AND FAIR

By the end of the nineteenth century, Detroit had grown to more than 205,000 people, nearly doubling in a decade, according to HistoricDetroit. org. Development had pushed north, east and west from lower Woodward Avenue, with new residential neighborhoods being built where corn fields and wooden lots once stood.

"The streets were paved with cobblestones and cedar blocks and the sidewalks were made of wood," noted Richard Bak in *HOUR Detroit*. "The widespread use of electricity was literally just around the corner—garish 125-foot towers illuminated intersections throughout the city—but for now, homes and businesses still used gaslight and trolleys were drawn by horses. Major symbols of progress—a new art museum, the city's first skyscraper, a second train depot—had either just opened or were under way."

Detroiters, fueled by the 1876 Centennial Exposition in Philadelphia, which was the country's first world's fair, were eager to show off this booming, modern town to the world, so they combined an agricultural fair with an industrial expo to create the Detroit International Exposition, which opened on September 17, 1889.

After city business leaders raised $500,000 in stocks to draw from, they bought seventy-two acres of land at the juncture of the Detroit and Rouge Rivers, near the Delray neighborhood, enjoyed by many fishermen, hunters and canoeists.

The marshes were drained and the farmland cleared, and then railroad tracks were laid directly into the grounds; two docks were built for excursion boats, according to *HOUR Detroit*. Then construction of the buildings began. The main expo building was grand but designed to be temporary, so it was constructed completely out of wood. It contained about 200,000 square feet of exhibition space and featured a tower offering views of the grounds. A *Harper's Weekly* article said that it was "the largest building in the world erected exclusively for fair and exposition purposes."

Hundreds of exhibitors signed up to show off their wares. Since this was before Detroit became Motor City, the industries displayed included items like stoves, soap, hoopskirts, railroad cars and seeds. It also had a painting gallery with three hundred works of art.

"Dozens chose to build small cottage-size structures at private expense all around the grounds, which were surrounded by a high fence," according

Main building, Detroit International Exposition, 1890. *HistoricDetroit.org.*

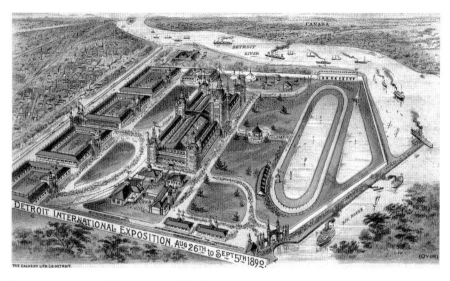

Detroit International Exposition, 1890. *HistoricDetroit.org*

to *HOUR Detroit*. "The livestock buildings also rapidly filled up. As opening day approached, a 'Babel of bleating, cackling, mooing, and grunting' arose from the stalls, which housed 'the finest breeds of cattle, sheep, swine, and poultry,' one daily paper reported. The final catalog of entries in the horse, cattle, and sheep categories alone filled 70 pages of fine print."

The Detroit Soap Company likely had the most fragrant cottage on the grounds, since the structure was carved from giant cakes of its popular Queen Anne soap, and the Pingree & Smith exhibit had busy workers demonstrating the art of making hundreds of pairs of shoes each day.

According to Historic Detroit, "The fair was so huge that Harper's Weekly wrote in its Aug. 17, 1889, issue ahead of the expo, that the only person capable of seeing everything in a day would be a 'professional pedestrian.'"

Admission was fifty cents for an adult and a quarter for a child. Besides the legal business taking place at the fair, there was plenty of illegal business occurring. "Law enforcement was a bit wobbly at first, with a night watchman (an ex-policeman) fired after he was caught pilfering merchandise from the Newcomb-Endicott exhibit the night before the fair's opening," reads *HOUR Detroit*. "That same evening, unknown persons sneaked onto the flatcar containing an out-of-state exhibitor's collection of West Indies coconut and banana trees and picked them clean of fruit. But after a few days, the sheriff in charge of the 70 uniformed officers assigned to the exposition grounds was able to report a quiet time of it. 'Everybody seems to be on his good behavior,' the sheriff noted. 'If there is a pickpocket or crook of any kind on the grounds, the detectives have been unable to find him.'"

Unusual side shows included a man who performed trapeze tricks while descending from the sky in a hot air balloon, a magician, a card-playing pig and trained seals and sea lions.

The expo's final day was September 27, and since more than 300,000 people had attended in those ten days, the organizers decided to bring it back each year. But after just a few years, attendance dropped, and the land was sold. According to Historic Detroit, in 1895 the Solvay Process Company, which produced soda ash for glassmaking, bought and cleared the grounds. Today, it is part of the heavily industrialized Zug Island in southwest Detroit.

BUFFALO'S PAN-AMERICAN EXPOSITION

A few years later, in May 1901, the Buffalo Pan-American Exposition opened its gates to visitors. Like the Detroit Expo, it had temporary exhibits displaying scientific and technological achievements in the region.

According to Thomas Leary, Elizabeth Sholes and the Erie County Historical Society's *Buffalo's Pan American Exposition*, "The decision to have the 1901 international exposition in Buffalo had many roots. The *Journal of American Industries* opined it was because Buffalo had 'a delightful climate… on account of the breezes from Lake Erie' and that the city was exceptionally healthful 'due somewhat to the fact that it has more asphalt pavements than any other city in the world' and 'an abundance of pure water from Lake Erie and an extensive and perfect drainage system with proper sanitary regulations well-enforced.' An important component to the site selection was the desire of the Niagara Frontier to show off its achievement in massive hydroelectric generation and long-distance transmission."

The Spanish-American War influenced the Pan-American theme. "The U.S. defeat of a Spanish presence in the Western Hemisphere, as well as areas of the Pacific such as the Philippines, opened the doors to a new era of exploitation of Central and South America and the Caribbean," according to *Buffalo's Pan-American Exposition*. "Thus, Exposition planners vowed that no nations outside the Western Hemisphere would have a presence within the formal exhibits."

It was originally planned to be built on Cayuga Island, but it was too remote for Buffalo residents. About twenty other locations were considered, with the Front—overlooking F.L. Olmsted's park system, Lake Erie and the Niagara

River—as the leading contender, but the area wasn't large enough. According to *Buffalo's Pan American Exposition*, the board decided on Rumsey Farm, near other park lands between Elmwood, Delaware and Forest Avenues.

Even though it wasn't on the lakefront, water still played an important role in its design. A mile-long canal went around the central buildings, broadening into two small ponds. There were also five hundred pieces of statuary, built by artists and craftsmen who emigrated from Italy to build them in five months.

Although two dozen men were involved in raising capital for the exposition, women played a big role in its development. A Board of Women Managers was established, consisting of society women, a newspaper reporter and business professionals. They were trivialized by the press, even though they were involved in recruiting exhibitors and promotions. They had a women's building on the expo grounds to "provide a haven for the 'New Woman' visitor to the Exposition," according to *Buffalo's Pan American Exposition*.

Women also played important roles in other aspects, including architect Josephine Wright Chapman, who won a sealed competition in Boston to design the New England Building, and S. Cecillia Cotter, who displayed her sculpture in the fine arts building. Numerous other women contributed as exhibitors, officers and technical and service employees.

Other expo buildings included the Temple of Music, Machinery and Transportation, Electricity, Ethnology, Manufactures and Liberal Arts and a Machinery Building, which contained a pumping station for the expo's fountains. It was oddly situated in the basement, where no one could see it, which displeased one of the engine's manufacturers, who complained to *American Machinist*, "The engines are down in a hole, and there is nothing to indicate that the hole exists, nor that it contains an engine exhibit."

It wasn't the only building garnering complaints. The Temple of Music was designed with elaborate carvings and painted in garish tones of red and salmon, and the nearby Ethnology Building contained a dizzying spiral staircase that inspired satirical sketches in local newspapers showing visitors disoriented by the stairs.

However, the expo's focal point was the Electrical Tower, which creators hoped would outdo the Eiffel Tower, built about a decade earlier for the 1889 exposition in Paris. "A cascade of water gushed from the tower, celebrating the harnessing of Niagara's cataracts for hydroelectric power generation," reads *Buffalo's Pan American Exposition*.

The hydraulic turbines and generators of the Niagara Falls Power Company produced the electricity that made the grounds glow brilliantly at night, according to the book:

Lighting became a design feature because of the recent electrical engineering innovations at Niagara Falls: generation of alternating current and its transmission over a considerable distance to Buffalo in 1896. According to a writer for the technical journal, Machinery, *"No such spectacle would be attempted anywhere else in the world at the present day. No such extravagant outlay of lights would be thought of where the power had to be furnished by coal and steam." Though hydroelectric power was transmitted greater distances in other regions such as California at the time of the Pan-Am, Buffalo still stood at the threshold of a new era in industrial and domestic applications of this novel power source.* Harper's Weekly *stated "Electrical Niagara is going to make Buffalo one of the largest manufacturing centers in the world."*

The lights were switched on each evening, and even Thomas Edison once watched the slow illumination on a late July night. The inventor exclaimed, "This is the apotheosis of incandescent light!"

According to *Buffalo's Pan American Exposition*, the *World's Work* correspondent Walter Hines Page described the ceremony:

You have hardly realized the scene as it appears in the dusk, when on the rows of posts tiny dots of light appear in clusters, like little pink buds in a nosegay. Then the pink points grow brighter and change their hue, and in another moment the full illumination bursts forth, and the whole great court becomes luminous with a soft brilliancy that does not tire the eye. And it is a new kind of brilliancy. You are face to face with the most magnificent and artistic nocturnal scene that man has ever made. I had the pleasure to see this illumination first in the company of a child of 10 years. She stood for a minute in speechless wonder. Then she cried, "Oh, isn't it beautiful!" And she danced in forgetfulness of herself and asked, "Is it really real?"

Visitors also enjoyed rides like the Aerio Cycle and other exciting features, including the Hyde Portable Fountain, a public water fountain, eliminating the common cups used at other taps around the expo. They were described by an article in the *New York Times*, saying how attractive was "this bending of the head above a sparkling little jet of water…to prevent the spread of contagious disease." The fountain won a medal for its ingenuity and was later installed in Buffalo's public schools.

In early September, fifty-eight-year-old President William McKinley and his wife, Ida, arrived at the expo to a waiting crowd of reporters and visitors. He was fresh off guiding the nation to victory in the Spanish-

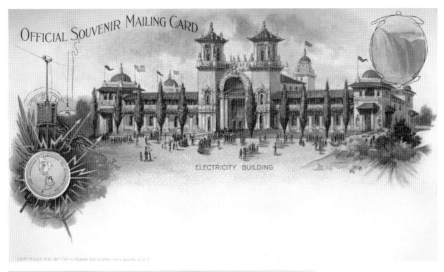

Above: Electricity Building, Pan-American Exposition, 1901. *Author's collection.*

Left: Aerio Cycle ride, Pan-Am Expo in Buffalo, New York, in 1901. *Author's collection.*

American War and entered his second term in office as one of the most popular presidents in decades.

"On September 5, a record crowd of 116,000 filed into the World's Fair to watch McKinley give a speech," according to Evan Andrews on History.com. "That same evening, the Expo put on patriotic fireworks display that culminated with a burst of pyrotechnics that spelled out the words, 'Welcome President McKinley, Chief of our Nation and Our Empire.'"

Andrews went on to say that McKinley's final expo appearance was a public meet-and-greet held at the Temple of Music the next day. According to the 1901 work *The True Story of the Assassination of President McKinley in Buffalo*, by Richard H. Barry, when he arrived at the temple, cheering crowds lined the way. After getting situated inside the building, he announced, "Let them come." The doors were opened, and people rushed in.

"[T]here appeared at the door—unnoticed at the time—a well-knit young man, whose right hand, with seeming innocence, was in his back pocket," wrote Barry. "That hand held a pistol, and both were concealed from even the treacherous depths of the pocket by a dirty rag. It was a handkerchief, plain, unmarked, ordinarily small and sorely soiled, yet it held the deadliest venom on Earth."

The man was twenty-eight-year-old Leon Czolgosz, a former steel worker and avowed anarchist, who moved down the line, inching closer to the president. When Czolgosz stood right in front of the president, McKinley was said to stick out his hand to shake his hand. Czolgosz had other plans; he raised his pistol, still wrapped in his handkerchief, and shot him.

"The first shot came, low—hardly louder than a cap pistol—then the second, as quick as the self-cocking trigger could work. A vague, startled thrill spread through the crowd." The president fell, and his marine guard charged the crowd with bayonets, driving them from the temple. A hush fell over the shocked crowd, and bystanders described the president as looking bewildered.

"The stillness was only broken when James 'Big Jim' Parker, a tall African American man who had been waiting in line, punched Czolgosz and prevented him from firing a third shot," wrote Andrews. "A host of soldiers and detectives also pounced on the assassin and began beating him to a pulp. It took an order from McKinley before they finally stopped and dragged Czolgosz from the room. By then, blood was pouring from the president's stomach and darkening his white formal vest. 'My wife,' he managed to say. 'Be careful how you tell her—oh, be careful!'"

McKinley was then carried from the Temple of Music to the expo hospital, where it was decided that he needed emergency surgery. In the

Temple of Music, Pan-American Exposition, 1901. *Author's collection.*

following days, he seemed to improve and was even alert but took a turn for the worse and died a week after the shooting, with his wife, Ida, at his side.

Three funerals were held, including one in Buffalo, where hundreds of thousands crowded the streets, but his final resting place is in Canton, Ohio. "The Temple of Music became the object of morbid curiosity and a shrine," reads *Buffalo's Pan American Exposition.*

The spot where McKinley stood was marked within fifteen minutes of the shooting; guards were posted, and a railing built around the site, to prevent splinters of the platform from being taken as souvenirs. "A visitor from Massillon, Ohio, noticed that the grain of the wood inside the rail resembled McKinley's profile, and crowds surged in to see the image."

Just a little over a month after the president's death, the expo was dealt another blow. "The board had sold stocks and bonds on the premise that 'the demand for concessions is an assurance of the success of the Exposition.' However, their elaborate plans based on a desire to outshine other expositions, cost more than estimated, and expenses outstripped revenues two-to-one. By Oct. 22, it was clear that only the original mortgage holders would receive any money. Contractors lost over $1 million for their work."

The board had a contract with Rumsey Farm saying that it would restore the land to what it looked like before the expo, so buildings were demolished, structures were removed and canals were filled in. By March 1902, the once vibrant property of the exposition had been reduced to ruins.

CLEVELAND'S GREAT LAKES EXPOSITION

Amid the Great Depression, the Great Lakes Exposition opened in Cleveland on June 27, 1936. It was one of the largest of the 1930s expositions, situated on a 135-acre site that stretched from two blocks northeast of Public Square to the intersection of East Twentieth Street and the lakeshore.

"The Exposition represents the endeavor of the people of Cleveland—in the centennial year of the incorporation of this community as a city—to express the material, social and cultural progress which has been achieved in the Great Lakes Region in the past 100 years," reads the 1936 Great Lakes Exposition Official Souvenir Guide.

A small group of Cleveland businessmen raised more than $1 million in loaned investments to develop the expo. The land was leased from the City of Cleveland, and in exchange, three permanent sites would remain from the expo, according to the booklet, including the Horticultural Building, Horticultural Gardens and East Ninth Street subway.

"Held along the lakefront on a reclaimed refuse dump, the Expo was intended to foster civic and regional pride, attract visitors and businesses to Cleveland, and provide an entertaining diversion in the midst of the Great Depression," according to the Cleveland Historical website.

"The topography of Cleveland's lakefront divides the Exposition grounds into three natural geographic sections. These divisions make the Great

1936 Great Lakes Exposition and Cleveland skyline. *Author's collection.*

Left: 1936 Great Lakes Exposition Official Souvenir Guide. *Author's collection.*

Below: 1937 Great Lakes Exposition souvenir ticket. *Author's collection.*

Left: 1936 Great Lakes Exposition flattened penny. *Author's collection.*

Below: Court of Presidents at Great Lakes Exposition, from souvenir guide. *Author's collection.*

Lakes Exposition the most clearly defined and the most easily understood exposition ever created. The grounds are divided naturally into the Upper Level, the Lower Level and the Amusement Section," reads the souvenir guide. "Passing between the towering pylons that identify the Main Entrance on St. Clair Avenue, just west of E. 6th Street, one enters the Upper Pavilion."

The seventy-seven-foot-tall pylons became an iconic image of the expo, featured on postcards, the souvenir booklet and even stamped pennies that were hand-cranked on site.

The Upper Pavilion contained Radioland, in Cleveland's Auditorium, which had hosted the Republican National Convention just several weeks earlier. It was converted and redecorated to become the world's largest broadcasting studio of the time.

The Great Lakes Symphony and Great Lakes Band played in the Symphony Shell on Sherwin-Williams Plaza. The Court of the Great Lakes contained model homes and replica historical cabins, like that of President James A. Garfield, who was born southeast of Cleveland and later raised his family at

Lawnfield in Mentor, Ohio, where the James A. Garfield National Historic Site still stands. The replica was based on the original cabin built in 1825 by Abram Garfield, grandfather of Abram Garfield, who was the supervising architect of the exposition. (The replica cabin from the expo now stands on the site of the Lake County Historical Society in Painesville. For years it was used in children's pioneer school but is now in need of repairs.)

The Upper Pavilion also contained the Lakeside Exhibition Hall, which exhibited industries of the Great Lakes, including the Romance of Iron and Steel.

After emerging from the north exits near the hall, visitors could descend to the Lower Level by crossing the "Court of Presidents." "A hundred booths line the sides of this broad bridge, bringing to it the historic atmosphere of the medieval European bridges," reads the souvenir booklet. "Sixteen of these booths, surmounted by huge eagles, honor the 16 presidents of the United States who were born in or elected from a Great Lakes state."

A Standard Drug building was on the Lower Level along with a large cafeteria, a large amphitheater, an enormous Automotive Building and the Hall of Progress and Municipal Stadium, where athletic demonstrations took place. The Horticultural Gardens were to the north, on the lakefront, along with the Horticultural Building, which showcased constantly changing flower shows. It was also the site where the luxurious nightclub *Showboat* was anchored, with twenty-five-cent admission during the day and fifty-cent admission in the evening.

"Its nationally famous orchestras provide dance music, while waiters in marine costumes serve the best food and drink," reads the 1936 booklet. "The Showboat is entered over a gangplank from the shore or by hanging ladder for those arriving by speed boat or yacht. The boat is 350 feet long and a veteran of the Great Lakes, having opened and closed the shipping season for many years. It has been entirely rebuilt, luxuriously furnished, and decorated to make it one of the country's most palatial night clubs."

The Lower Level also featured a towering Higbee Building, singing fountains in front of the Firestone Building and a tropical Florida Exhibit Building.

Visitors entered the Amusement Midway section through the East Ninth Street entrance on the eastern side of the Lower Level. The souvenir guide describes its variety of entertainment:

> *Many of the famous circus, theatrical and spectacular outdoor attractions of the Western World are gathered here. Rides of every type provide thrills*

and entertainment. Strange and fascinating sights abound. Visitors may choose from Shakespearian plays, a submarine visit, fishing, dancing, motor boating, blimp rides over the lakefront. Fireworks displays shoot from barges in the lake, several nights weekly. At the eastern end of the Amusement Sections is Streets of the World with its myriad cafes, displays of foreign goods, and night life that provides a world tour.

On the waterfront, visitors could fly in a seaplane or the Goodyear blimp to see the expo from above or admire it from the shoreline aboard a speed boat or paddleboat.

According to the souvenir booklet, other amusements included:

- Monkey Land, where monkeys raced cars in the loop-the-loop in a jungle atmosphere.
- Spook Street had "weird thrills including a ghost dinner."
- Lion Motordrome consisted of live lions and motorcycle riders speeding along a perpendicular wall and doing daredevil stunts.
- A television, which was very new technology, allowed visitors to stand under a photo cell block to see a reproduction of themselves "three times life size."

The expo also had entertainment that was not family-friendly, including nudity, particularly in the Streets of the World section at the east end of the Midway.

"Attending the Exposition required a financial commitment, especially in the middle of the Great Depression," wrote Brad Schwartz in *The 1936–1937 Great Lakes Exposition*. "[N]early all of the Exposition's attendees were well-dressed Caucasians. Partly because it was the 1930s and partly because the Exposition was an 'event,' the dress code was summer dresses and heels for women and jackets and ties for men. There were very few children in attendance, especially during its first year, when nudity and questionable entertainment abounded."

According to Schwartz, most of the expo's attractions required an additional entrance fee (from $0.15 to see the monkeys to $3 to ride in a blimp). Including the cost of food and souvenirs, a trip to the expo could range from $6 to $15, which is equal to $100 to $250 in today's dollars.

The 1936 expo season was only supposed to run one hundred days, but it was not as financially successful as organizers hoped, so they decided to open it again the following summer to try to increase their profit. When it reopened at the end of May 1937, some of its least successful attractions had been closed and replaced.

1936 airplane view of Lower Level of Great Lakes Exposition, from souvenir guide. *Author's collection.*

"One of the 1937 additions was a huge floating stage and a lake-water pool that featured Billy Rose's Aquacade, a music, dance, and swimming show that starred Johnny Weissmuller of Tarzan fame, and Olympic gold medalist Eleanor Holm," wrote Schwartz. "Although it was forbidden by Exposition organizers during the second year, a few of the Expo's 1937 attractions tried off and on to draw people in by offering female nudity, but their efforts were quickly checked."

Although the two seasons weren't a financial success, the expo drew positive attention and offered visitors a diversion when they needed it.

Only a few of the more than 150 expo buildings were meant to be permanent, and today nothing remains at the site. "The two features that were intended to be permanent additions to the city's lakefront did not last," noted Schwartz. "The Horticulture Building burned down in the early 1940s, and the Horticultural Gardens waned until they were removed to make way for the Cleveland Browns' new stadium." (Statues and fountains from the gardens remained along the waterfront for years but were eventually removed, and some were relocated to other Cleveland gardens.)

Burke Lakefront Airport, the Rock-and-Roll Hall of Fame, the Great Lakes Science Center and Cleveland Browns Stadium now stretch across the site that was transformed for two summers into the Great Lakes Exposition.

TRAILBLAZERS
AND LEGENDARY TALES

"FRENCHY THE PIRATE," OF FAIRPORT

For many years, there has been a legend along the shores of Fairport Harbor, Ohio, of a man known as "Frenchy the Pirate," who lived in a shack on the beach. The shack is long gone, but the legend lives on; it turns out he wasn't only folklore after all.

Frenchy was said to arrive in the quaint town on the night of a tempestuous storm. His ship splintered on the beach, and he was resourceful enough to use the wood to build his home. He's been called a "waterfront character," simply "the Pirate" and a "squatter," among other things. According to stories passed down by generations, he seems to fit them all.

Saul Ollila's *Hometown Sketches* reads, "[L]ittle is known of this colorful sailor. Reticent and alone, he lived in a shack on the local beach with a pack of about twenty bull dogs."

In this new town, Frenchy became the village peddler, selling Lake Erie water for twenty-five cents per barrel. (This was before a water system was installed and few people had wells, so fresh water was likely worth the price.)

"The pirate's horse and wagon full of splashing barrels of water, followed by a pack of bulldogs, was a familiar sight in Fairport at the turn of the century," according to Ollila. "Later the old sailor sold sand on the beach."

He was said to be a mutineer and pirate on the high seas before arriving in Fairport and was known to keep to himself. A 1914 *Painesville Telegraph-*

PIER AND LIFEBOAT-HOUSE, FAIRPORT.

This sketch may depict Frenchy the Pirate on the beach of Fairport, Ohio. *Lee Silvi, source unknown.*

Republican article, written after his death, shared these details about his vagabond adventures:

> *When a small boy he left his home in France by the runaway route, shipping on a sea-going boat bound for this country which landed him in Savannah during the Civil War.*
>
> *According to "Frenchy," he was forcibly made to enter the Confederate navy. He served on various gunboats until his clothes were reduced to shreds and he was disgusted with the life. Trouble with an officer brought things to a climax. The officer received the blows, which "Frenchy" handed in his direction.*
>
> *"Frenchy" knowing that to strike an officer was a serious offense, immediately took "French" leave of the navy.*

He made his way to a nearby port and hid as a stowaway on an outgoing boat loaded with cotton. He spent time in Australia during the gold rush and accrued a large amount of money working in the mining camps. Next Frenchy spent years as a seaman on ships sailing the Great Lakes "until his age went up against him and he was compelled to give it up."

According to the 1914 article, that was when he washed ashore, building his home on "the Huntington property without asking permission, thereby becoming a squatter":

A part of the structure was made from a section of a boat while the remainder was built from wreckage. The interior of the cabin was furnished from the wreckage. Chairs, beds, etc. were taken from the beach. "Frenchy" was a neat housekeeper, things being in order at all times. Every morning he "washed down the decks." This was done by throwing a pail of water on the floor and scouring it with lake sand.

It goes on to say that sometimes Frenchy refused to talk, but other times he talked all about the customs he knew about pirates in different countries:

This, with the fact that he bore an ugly looking scar on one side of his face, might be exceedingly interesting.

For a number of years "Frenchy" worked on the docks at Fairport but the later years were spent at his cabin where visitors, as a rule, were not given a very cordial welcome. The deceased is survived by one sister who is in a convent in France.

Years later, local historians, volunteers and members of the Fairport Harbor Marine Museum and Lighthouse Lee Silvi and Bob Manross wanted to find the truth about Frenchy. After examining countless historic Fairport maps, they believe that Frenchy's shack was on Fairport Beach, near the current Lake Metroparks pavilion, as the Huntington property was in that same area.

One day, they were both, unknowingly, searching for Frenchy's grave at Painesville, Ohio's historic Evergreen Cemetery within a few hours of each other (which they discovered later due to a social media post made by Silvi). Lori Pike Watson, treasurer and historian of the LeRoy Heritage Association, helped by finding and sharing Frenchy's death certificate, which lists his full name as "Frank Thompson" and his birthplace and parents' names as "unknown." It says he died on July 19, 1914, at the age of "about 75."

"We discovered his grave was not marked," wrote Silvi in a Facebook post about their venture. "Together we set out to correct this matter, by obtaining a marker for the grave. Bob was the first to obtain a donated gravestone, and also handled the process of getting the permit to mark the grave site. The

Frenchy the Pirate's grave marker. *Lee Silvi.*

cost of pouring the footer for the marker was paid by the two of us to the City of Painesville."

The grave marker, engraving and installation were donated by Ron Belding Monuments of Geneva, Ohio.

On November 28, 2022, the marker was placed on Frenchy's grave site (in Division 18, Lot 33 Evergreen Cemetery), more than a century after his death.

His story is what legends are made of, pieced together and outlandish, yet he was a real man, who will now always be remembered, as the words written across his grave marker read, "Frank Thompson, Fairport Harbor's 'Frenchy the Pirate' 1838–1914."

MESSAGE IN A BOTTLE

On June 30, 1915, two young women from Detroit, enjoying a summer day at Tashmoo Park, decided to write a message. Selina Pramstaller and Tillie Esper wrote on a piece of paper, "Having a good time at Tashmoo." They stuffed their note in a bottle, pushed in the cork and threw it in the St. Clair River.

The bottle and its message were discovered nearly a century later in 2012 by diver Dave Leander, according to an article by Christina Hall in the 2013 *Detroit Free Press.* Leander, the owner of Great Lakes DiveCenter Inc., in Shelby Township, found the bottle tucked in about six inches of dirt, in thirty feet of water near the location where the Tashmoo steamship used to dock when it ferried passengers to Tashmoo Park.

Leander brought the bottle home to show his wife, and they noticed that the bottle was discovered almost exactly to the date the message

Tashmoo Park dock, St. Clair Flats, 1905. *Library of Congress.*

was written ninety-seven years before. They decided not to remove the message, written in a neat cursive writing, but instead let the bottle dry out and replaced the cork.

According to the article, the Leanders asked their diver friend Michael Brodzik about the bottle. His experience as the president of the Metropolitan Detroit Antique Bottle Club helped them determine that the bottle likely contained cherries or olives before it was emptied and sank where the women threw it because it wasn't buoyant enough to float.

Brodzik explained in the article, "There was a little air in the bottle when it was found, a touch of dampness, with part of the paper sticking to the bottle."

Brodzik, his brother Joe and sister-in-law Jenni searched genealogy records, city directories and census records to learn about Pramstaller and Esper and track down their descendants.

Several years later, according to Christina Hall's July 16, 2015 *Detroit Free Press* article, they did indeed find family members, who were planning to travel to Harsens Island, where Tashmoo Park once existed, for the annual

Tashmoo Days, to "remember Pramstaller and Esper, their message, the beloved excursion steamship, the once-thriving park, and the memories made there."

BLANCHE WILCOX NOYES AND
THE FIRST WOMEN'S AIR DERBY

At a time when flying an airplane was considered a man's job, plenty of women were determined to break barriers and soar.

Blanche Wilcox Noyes of Lakewood, a suburb west of Cleveland, was a striking brunette who started out as a stage actress performing at Gordon Square Theater, but she was much more than just a pretty face. Noyes wanted to fly. She earned her pilot's license in the late 1920s, making her Ohio's first aviatrix.

According to a *Washington Post* article, a year after she and her husband, Dewey Noyes, were married in 1928, he bought her a plane and taught her

Blanche Noyes (*standing second from right*) with Louise Thaden (believed to be sitting on running board on the far left) and seven other participants of the 1929 Women's Air Derby. *International Women's Air & Space Museum, Cleveland, Ohio.*

how to fly. (He had a background in flying as the chief pilot of the Standard Oil Company, in Ohio, and a former airmail flier, according to the Museum of Women Pilots.)

He also helped her prepare for the first women's air derby, from Santa Monica to Cleveland, called the National Women's Air Derby of 1929 (named the "Powder Puff Derby" by some male reporters covering the event).

She flew her Travel Air biplane, *Miss Cleveland*, over nine days and 2,800 miles with the other pilots. In the 1920s, women pilots were often seen as oddities or opportunists, so the derby gave them a chance to prove their skills in the air and be taken seriously as pilots.

"The pistol shot that started the race on August 18, 1929, was fired in Cleveland, relayed by radio, carried over loudspeakers to the race's starting location at Clover Field, then signaled to each woman by an official starter with the lowering of a flag," reads an article on the National Aviation Heritage Area website. "The women took off at one- to two-minute intervals with squadrons of planes carrying race officials and press following."

"It featured some of the best women pilots in the world, with strict qualifications," according to JSTOR Daily. "The women had to have at least 100 solo flying hours, 25 of those being long distance (over 40 miles); each plane had to be licensed by the Department of Commerce; each woman had to wear a parachute; and each had to carry a gallon of water and food for three days."

"Mechanical troubles, sabotage, curious spectators, lack of sleep, and sickness were all hazards the women had to face," reads the National Aviation Heritage Area website. "Most of these women were flying in open-cockpit planes bearing the full heat and dust of late summer. Navigation tools were limited to looking for landmarks, following road maps, and flying along rail lines. The lower the pilots flew, however, the closer they were to dangerous telephone lines, buildings, and uneven terrain."

"The 1929 derby was brutal," according to Becky Boban of *Cleveland Magazine*. "Navigation by 'dead reckoning' was only the start of Noyes' problems when she inadvertently landed in Mexico. Flying to El Paso, a smoldering cigarette caught fire in the cabin near the engine."

Noyes side-slipped two thousand feet, fell quickly and smacked into three-foot mesquite bushes, ripping her plane's fire extinguisher from its screws, which then failed to work. She ended up smothering the flames with sand; as Boban explained, her plane arrived in Pecos resembling a wounded duck. "Noyes was able to find a blacksmith who was willing to weld the damaged landing rig while the pilot spent most of her night sewing the plane's wing together with fabric before taking off the next day," added Boban.

The National Women's Air Derby was scheduled to end at the Cleveland National Air Races (predecessor of the Cleveland Air Show) at Cleveland Municipal Airport (now Cleveland Hopkins International). It featured closed-course races around pylons, along with several men's cross-country airplane races, aerial acrobatics shows, blimp rides and even an appearance by aviator Charles Lindbergh. About 300,000 people paid two dollars per ticket for the festivities, according to the National Aviation Heritage Area website, which included seeing the women finish the derby.

On that summer day on August 26, Noyes flew into Cleveland and finished fourth, right behind Amelia Earhart, to a boisterous welcome of loud cheers and applause. She later told the *Plain Dealer*, "I think I've autographed everything but flypaper." She was one of fourteen, out of the original twenty, to complete the race.

Louise Thaden, who finished first in the heavy class (there was also a light class), was quoted as saying, "We think we have done something toward proving that women have a place in the air."

The derby kindled a friendship between Earhart and Noyes that led to her connecting with the old Bureau of Air Commerce, a predecessor of the Civil Aeronautics Authority and Federal Aviation Administration, for which Earhart helped establish an air marking program. A *Washington Post* article notes that Noyes made air safety her top priority and joined the bureau in 1936, and over her thirty-five-year government career, she arranged for thousands of cities and towns to display their names on rooftops and completed about seventy-five thousand air markings (like road signs for air travel) across the country.

"The markings, large yellow and black painted arrows with the mileage to the nearest airport, were used to guide pilots in their flight," reads the article. She came up with the idea after her husband died in a plane crash in 1935.

She was among the first women pilots in the United States and for years the government's only official woman flyer, crisscrossing the country many times in the interest of air safety. She also wrote air marking textbooks and designed air markers. She was co-winner, with fellow pioneering aviatrix Louise Thaden, of the Bendix speed dash in 1936 and competed in every national air race for women, except one, setting the women's east–west speed record of fourteen hours, fifty-four minutes and forty-nine seconds. She even took business mogul John D. Rockefeller, at ninety years old, on his first and only air ride in 1930, according to the *Washington Post*.

She loved her work and was once quoted as saying, "In the air I feel above all petty things; it's like a religion with me."

During World War II, Noyes worked for the War Department, teaching new military pilots, and was a charter member of the Ninety-Nines Inc., an international organization of women pilots, which she cofounded with Amelia Earhart. She was inducted into the Aviation Hall of Fame in 1970 and was the first woman to receive a gold medal from the Commerce Department.

The aviation pioneer died at the age of eighty-one in Washington, but she is still inspiring many today to look up to the sky and soar among the clouds just like she once did.

ST. JOE'S RADIO CLUB: TRACKING SPUTNIK

The 1950s and '60s epitomized the era of the "space race" between Cold War rivals the United States and Soviet Union. The prospect of being the first to conquer space exploration fueled imaginations and had our nation on the edge of its seat.

However, when you think of the space race, you likely don't think of Ohio or the students at a small, Catholic high school on the shores of Lake Erie as playing a role in it. But they did.

It all started in the heyday of ham radio at the St. Joe's Radio Club (with call letters W8KTZ) at St. Joseph High School in Cleveland. Between 1951 and 1979, more than 150 students at the all-boys school got their ham radio licenses, learned Morse code and built and repaired ham radio equipment through that club.

They "performed public-service work, such as providing communications for special events, conducting Halloween Vandal Patrols, participating in Civil Defense drills and RACES—the Radio Amateur Communications Emergency Service," according to the St. Joe's Radio Club commemorative website.

On the evening of October 4, 1957, the radio club was on the brink of making an incredible discovery. The group's leader, Mike Stimac, religious brother and teacher at the school, received a phone call from club member John Van Blargan: "A TV news report said the Russians have put something into space which is transmitting a signal on 20 Megacycles. Do you know anything about it?"

Mike relayed the story in his book, *The Visionary Life & World Adventures of Mike Stimac*. Mike told him he hadn't heard of it and asked John if the signal would keep going until morning. "I don't know," John responded. "Can you meet us at the lab? We're hearing something near that frequency. We hear it for about 20 minutes, then everything is quiet for about 70 minutes before we hear it again. We have been recording it."

The exciting news quickly spread among members overnight, and the next morning, they were already there on their ham radio receiver searching for the mysterious Russian signal.

"More kids kept arriving," wrote Mike. "The lab was not a school place, it was an island of adventure and Saturday morning was simply a fully free time to enjoy it. But on this particular morning there was a mystery to solve. The gang was looking to outer space for clues."

Club members heard news reports saying that the signal was heard just above WWV government beacon, broadcast on short-wave radio (whose signal could be heard at twenty megacycles), yet they weren't sure why the Russian signal only occurred periodically.

John said, "It sounds like a chirp. Little bursts of teletype signal would sound like that."

The group watched the radio dial, just below the fifteen-meter frequencies. Suddenly everyone's attention was on a faint chirping sound coming from the receiver. It grew stronger, reached a peak and then faded.

Ed Miller rotated the antenna to follow the signal, which was strongest when it was pointed northwest and then had to be rotated to the south before it faded and disappeared.

Bernie Kulwin mentioned, "A news reporter said that Russians had put something out in space that was circling the Earth. The reporter called it a 'satellite' and said it was 'in orbit around the Earth.'"

The group realized if that was what they were hearing it was moving from north to south, and they should be able to pick up the signal again after it traveled around Earth.

About ninety minutes later, the chirping noise came back again faintly. The students switched on their big ten-inch reel Berlant Concertone tape machine to record the chirps from the mysterious transmitter in outer space.

Tom Hipp began recording the length of time they heard the chirping noise and antenna directions on the blackboard. Mike Cegelski marked sections of tracked orbit with ribbons of paper on a twelve-inch globe and realized that the orbits appeared parallel but were moving west.

Joe Marsey commented, "You would get this same pattern if the transmitting object or satellite travelled in a flat circle and the earth was spinning around inside the circle."

This made Mike quickly realize that it was like a gyroscope: "The path of the satellite is like the fixed frame outside in space and the earth is like the inner spinning part. So, the orbit is not moving west, it is the earth and us who are moving east."

Using the amount of time it took the satellite to orbit Earth and rotation of the planet, the group realized they could calculate where to look for the satellite next. "The young scientists, with their radio signal expertise, were already solving a mystery that the rest of the world was wondering about," wrote Mike.

The group scheduled listening times and developed a tracking device, the "orbitometer," a circular slide rule that allowed them to calculate future satellite paths in orbit.

Club member Fred Imm checked the data and realized that a satellite pass from Moscow to Cleveland took sixteen minutes. "I was impressed," wrote Mike. "The original thinking being done by this group was astounding. I felt that they were ready to join any scientific research team around the world."

The group decided that this would certainly interest news organizations, so they called the *Cleveland Press* and asked if they would like information about the Russian satellite. "Absolutely!" the reporter responded. "But everybody is finding it pretty mysterious so what's happening out there?"

"Well, there is no mystery for us," Mike told him. "We have figured out that it is in an orbit that we have nailed down, and so we know to the minute when we can pick up the signal and from what direction."

The *Press* responded, "Well, nobody has come up with that yet, so it sounds kind of unbelievable."

Mike agreed but offered to let the reporter listen to the chirping noise over the phone when the satellite was scheduled to go by that afternoon.

At 3:22 p.m., right on schedule, the chirping sound came, and the reporter responded, "Wow, is that the actual signal?"

Mike responded, "Yes, that's it! We have a load of tape recordings, and it is following our figures so closely that it leaves no doubt."

The *Press* sent out a crew to get photos and more information, and the St. Joe's Radio Club was catapulted into the public eye. WEWS-TV wanted the club to do a live demonstration in the studio on the 11:00 p.m. news. They did such a great job that the station manager told Mike afterward, "Never saw anything like it. These kids act like they do this every day."

Mike replied, "Actually they do. They talk to people all over the world on our amateur radio station."

Several members of the St. Joe's Radio Club, the "Sputnik gang," October 1957. *Photo by Michael Stimac and contributed by Robert Leskovec.*

The next day, club members noticed that there was a break in the rhythmic cadence of the chirp. The group again contacted the news because it could mean that the transmitter was wearing out or failing. The operator at the wire services thanked them for the information and said, "It's on the wire. You'll hear it on the news stations in a few minutes."

Of course, they tuned in, and this is what they heard:

There is developing news about the Russian satellite, Sputnik. Observers are reporting that the signal is breaking up. No one knows what is wrong, but any number of things may be happening. The transmitter equipment itself may be failing, or the satellite may be dropping down into the atmosphere and beginning to break up. We do know for certain that the signal is changing. This has been reported by MIT Lincoln labs in Boston, the Bureau of Standards in Boulder, Colorado, the Naval Observatory in Washington, and the Saint Joseph's High Radio Club in Cleveland.

The kids were thrilled to be included among the top scientists and researchers in the country! If that wasn't exciting enough, several weeks later, two men from the FBI, dressed in black suits and dark sunglasses, arrived at the radio lab.

The radio station was suddenly turned off, and the room went quiet. Everyone feared that something very bad had happened. The young amateur radio operators knew that they were dealing with powerful radio transmitters which, if not carefully controlled, could interfere with television sets, taxicab communications, air traffic control or emergency communications. Yet the boys had been trained to operate at the station safely, passing government exams and getting their licenses.

"Are you the group that has been tracking the satellite since it went up?" Mike recalled one FBI agent asking. "We believe your group began tracking the satellite four hours before the Naval Observatory of the government did. They lost some vital clues about orbit decay in those hours. Your tapes will fill in the gap."

After the agents left with five of their ten-inch reels of recording tape, the questions began flying. Club member Bob Leskovec said, "At first I thought the guy must be joking. They had to come to a high school radio lab for data? The Naval Observatory must have every kind of radio equipment because they communicate with ships and submarines and do all those atmospheric measurements. How could they not find a single antenna and a receiver that would tune in the satellite?" They never got an answer.

But the group continued to gain attention and ended up being featured in *CQ Amateur Radio* magazine. Leskovec noticed that one of their oscilloscope images, showing the waveforms of the Sputnik signal, was on the front cover of the January 1958 issue, and their story, submitted by Stimac, was featured inside.

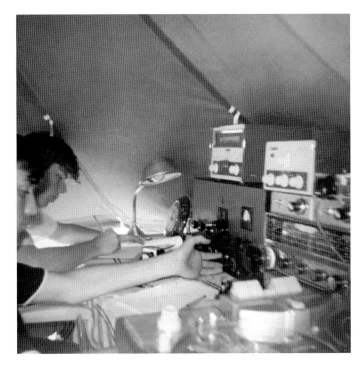

Anthony Emanuele and my dad, Dale Boresz, participating in the Amateur Radio Relay League 1968 Field Day (emergency simulation) event. *Dale Boresz.*

The students made it on dozens of TV shows, radio news stories and newspaper articles, and a teaching aid company took notice of their "orbitometer" and arranged with the high school to secure a patent and produce it as an educational device. It was the first satellite slide rule, so the patent was immediately granted, but it wasn't produced commercially so the club never made money on its creation.

The club inspired younger kids who had their sights set on St. Joe's to join the infamous radio club, like my dad, Dale Boresz, and his childhood friend Anthony Emanuele, who grew up across the street from him in the eastern Cleveland suburb of Wickliffe. They both became interested in radio and ham radio in elementary school and have fond memories of walking up to the Wickliffe Public Library each Saturday to check out everything they could on radio, including magazines featuring the radio club.

"We knew about the club's Sputnik involvement because of what we read from going to the library all the time," my dad told me. "I wanted to join the club before I ever got out of grade school. That was the goal, if possible: go to St. Joe's so I could join the radio club."

He and Anthony both ended up attending St. Joe's and joining the radio club. "It reinforced my interest in electronics, communication, radio and technology, which I continue to enjoy with my involvement with amateur radio today." And he and Anthony have stayed friends through the years. They enjoy communicating via ham radio, including their scheduled weekly chat, which has been going on for decades.

The students graduated, and the St. Joe's Radio Club eventually disbanded. In 1990, St. Joseph High School merged with Villa Angela Academy to become Villa Angela–St. Joseph High School.

Yet the club launched a lot of its members' careers. Students later worked as chief engineers in radio and TV, university professors and science teachers, medical doctors and members of the military working in defense. My dad went on to be a computer programmer, small business owner and entrepreneur.

Little did those high school students know, as they worked together to figure out the source behind a mere beep, how their actions would inspire and intrigue so many for years to come, proving that you're never too old, or too young, to make a lasting impact.

EPILOGUE

Millions of people live along Lake Erie's shores—on islands, in small towns and in major cities. This Midwest region was built by hardworking pioneers, innovators and business men and women—people who have dreamed big and been willing to take even larger risks.

Even though the businesses and industries mentioned in this book no longer exist, they helped develop our communities and became an important piece of our history. The Rust Belt cities have seen a rise and

Lake Erie sunset in western Lake County, Ohio. *Photo by author.*

fall in manufacturing over the years, and while some areas are still littered with empty factories, others are rebuilding and excelling in new industries.

Lake Erie has been at the center of it all—a source of joy, heartache and mystery. When you look out at the vast water of the lake, it may be sparkling blue, gray with white-capped waves or illuminated with the vibrant colors of a sunrise or sunset, but despite the changes forever happening in and around it, it remains at the very heart of our region—a constant, just like its waves, beating as rhythmically as a heartbeat, crashing in and rolling back out.

BIBLIOGRAPHY

Albrecht, Brian. "Saga of Ashtabula Train Disaster Endures After 140 Years." *Cleveland Plain Dealer*, December 28, 2016. https://www.cleveland.com/metro/2016/12/saga_of_ashtabula_train_disast.html.

American Rails. "Shay Steam Locomotive." https://www.american-rails.com/shay.html.

Andrews, Evan. "The Assassination of President William McKinley." History, September 3, 2018. https://www.history.com/news/the-assassination-of-president-william-mckinley.

Atlas Obscura. "Site of the Angola Horror: Angola, New York." June 25, 2020. https://www.atlasobscura.com/places/angola-horror.

Austin, Dan. "Tashmoo." Historic Detroit. https://historicdetroit.org/buildings/tashmoo.

Bak, Richard. "A Fair to Remember." *HOUR Detroit* (January 22, 2009). https://www.hourdetroit.com/community/a-fair-to-remember.

Barry, Richard H. *The True Story of the Assassination of President McKinley at Buffalo*. Buffalo, NY: Robert Alan Reid, 1901.

Beach Combing. "Black Sea Glass" (February 12, 2019). https://www.beachcombingmagazine.com/blogs/news/black-sea-glass.

Beahan, Larry. "A One Tank Trip to Barcelona Harbor." Westfield, New York, August 2010. https://westfieldny.com/visiting/one-tank-trip-barcelona-harbor.

Binion, Stefan. "Lake Erie Park and Casino: A Text Adventure." Midstory, June 16, 2020. https://www.midstory.org/lake-erie-park-and-casino-a-text-adventure.

Boban, Becky. *Cleveland Magazine* Facebook article, March 2023. https://www.facebook.com/profile/100046908535235/search/?q=blanche%20wilcox%20noyes.

Brady, Dan. "Brady's Bunch of Lorain County Nostalgia." Blog, May 28, 2021. https://danielebrady.blogspot.com/2021/05/lake-road-inn-ad-may-27-1924.html.

Brock University Library, Archives and Special Collections. "The Americana and Canadiana." https://exhibits.library.brocku.ca/s/Crystal/page/the-canadiana-and-americana.

Chip, June E. "Erie Beach Park—Rides and Remnants." Western New York Heritage, March 30, 2022. https://www.wnyheritage.org/content/erie_beach_park--_rides_and_remnants/index.html.

Cichon, Steve. "Out of the Past: The Circle Inn, Athol Springs." Blog, March 3, 2017. http://blog.buffalostories.com/tag/athol-springs.

The City of Erie, PA. Erie, PA: Herald Printing and Publishing Company, 1888.

Cleveland Historical. "The Great Lakes Exposition: Two Summers of Excitement." https://clevelandhistorical.org/items/show/71.

Cleveland Memory. "The Hulett Automatic Ore Unloaders Online." http://www.clevelandmemory.org/glihc/hulett/index.html.

Cleveland Plain Dealer. "Cleveland's New Lighthouse Park Shows How Small Urban Spaces Can Create Magic." August 2022.

Conlin, John H. "The Famous Central Wharf of the Buffalo Waterfront: Part I." Western New York Heritage, April 4, 2016. https://www.wnyheritage.org/content/the_famous_central_wharf_of_the_buffalo_waterfront_part_i/index.html.

———. "The Famous Central Wharf of the Buffalo Waterfront: Part II." Western New York Heritage, April 5, 2016. https://www.wnyheritage.org/content/the_famous_central_wharf_of_the_buffalo_waterfront_part_i/index.html.

———. "The Famous Central Wharf of the Buffalo Waterfront: Part III." Western New York Heritage, April 6, 2016. https://www.wnyheritage.org/content/the_famous_central_wharf_of_the_buffalo_waterfront_part_iii/index.htmle.

Detroit Free Press. "City of Erie Won Big Race by Only 45 Seconds." June 5, 1901.

———. "Magnificent Fast Excursion Steamer Tashmoo Launched Yesterday." December 31, 1899.

Discover Vermilion. "1877 Vermilion Lighthouse." February 6, 2023. https://www.discoververmilion.org/news-and-events/news/params/post/4139105/1877-vermilion-lighthouse.

———. "The History of Crystal Beach." November 26, 2022. https://www.discoververmilion.org/news-and-events/news/params/post/4139125/the-history-of-crystal-beach.

Eby, David L. "History of Toledo Beach Amusement Park." *Monroe News*, October 19, 2020. https://www.monroenews.com/story/news/history/2020/10/19/history-of-toledo-beach-amusement-park/42856209.

Encyclopedia of Cleveland History, Case Western Reserve University. "*Aquarama*." https://case.edu/ech/articles/a/aquarama.

———. "Bolton, Charles Chester." https://case.edu/ech/articles/b/bolton-charles-chester.

———. "Cleveland Municipal Stadium." https://case.edu/ech/articles/c/cleveland-municipal-stadium.

———. "Hulett, George H." https://case.edu/ech/articles/h/hulett-george-h

———. "Hulett Ore Unloaders." https://case.edu/ech/articles/h/hulett-ore-unloaders.

Euclid Beach Park Now. *Euclid Beach Park*. Charleston, SC: Arcadia Publishing, 2012.

Exploring Niagara. "Crystal Beach Amusement Park." https://www.exploringniagara.com/places_to_explore/forgotten_places/crystal_beach_amusement_park.html.

———. "Erie Beach Amusement Park." https://www.exploringniagara.com/places_to_explore/forgotten_places/erie_beach_amusement_park.html.

Feather, Carl E. *Ashtabula Harbor, Ohio: A History of the World's Greatest Iron Ore Receiving Port*. N.p.: CreateSpace Independent Publishing Platform, 2017.

———. "Mr. Hulett's Invention." *Star Beacon*, March 25, 2012. https://www.starbeacon.com/community/mr-hulett-s-invention/article_2b7aaf70-7cd2-5279-b739-9a5e7b23fc33.html.

Flagdom. "Commodore Perry Flag." https://flagdom.com/historical-flags/commodore-perry-flag.

Fleming, Roy F. "Abigail Becker: Heroine of Long Point, Lake Erie, October 1946." National Museum of the Great Lakes. https://nmgl.org/abigail-becker-heroine-of-long-point-lake-erie-october-1946.

Fraser, Chad. *Lake Erie Stories: Struggle and Survival on a Freshwater Ocean*. Toronto, CAN: Dundurn Press, 2008.

Frew, David. *Midnight Herring: Prohibition and Rum Running on Lake Erie*. Erie, PA: Erie County Historical Society and Museum, 2006.

Gebhart, Richard. *Ships and Shipwrecks: Stories from the Great Lakes*. East Lansing, MI: Greenstone Books, 2021.

Glaser, Cris. "Memories of McGarvey's." *Morning Journal*, July 16, 2021. https://www.morningjournal.com/2000/10/08/memories-of-mcgarveys/#.

Goldstein, Alan. "Queen of the Inland Seas." *Thousand Islands Life* 17, no. 4 (April 2022). https://thousandislandslife.com/queen-of-the-inland-seas.

Great Lakes Guide. "Lake Erie." https://greatlakes.guide/watersheds/erie.

Haggart, Greg, and Nancy Haggart. *Pirates of the Great Lakes*. Morrisville, NC: Lulu Publishing, 2008.

Hall, Christina. "Note in Bottle Written by Girls Resurfaces After 97 Years." *Detroit Free Press*, June 18, 2013.

———. "Tashmoo Days on Harsens Island Offer a Trip Back in Time." *Detroit Free Press*, July 16, 2015.

Hall, Stephanie. "Who Were Those Gals?: 'Buffalo Gals' Revisited." *Library of Congress Blogs*, August 17, 2020. https://blogs.loc.gov/folklife/2020/08/buffalo-gals-revisited-2.

Hayden, Brian. "Afternoon Drive: Fresh Fish, an Ode to the Past at Westfield Fisheries." *Buffalo News*, September 15, 2020. https://buffalonews.com/entertainment/afternoon-drive-fresh-fish-an-ode-to-the-past-at-westfield-fisheries/article_538318d0-f6b7-11ea-b992-f3cef050c776.html.

Historic Detroit. "International Exposition Building." https://historicdetroit.org/buildings/international-exposition-building.

History. "Hundreds Drown in Eastland Disaster." November 13, 2009. https://www.history.com/this-day-in-history/hundreds-drown-in-eastland-disaster.

Jackson, Ashawnta. "1929 Women's Air Derby Changed Views on Women Pilots." JSTOR Daily, March 8, 2022. https://daily.jstor.org/1929-womens-air-derby-changed-views-on-women-pilots.

Johnson's Island. http://johnsonsisland.org.

Johnston, Laura. "Cleveland Municipal Stadium Is Underwater in Lake Erie: Remember When." Rock the Lake, January 3, 2018. http://www.rockthelake.com/buzz/2018/01/cleveland-municipal-stadium-underwater-lake-erie.

———. "The Mystery of Bricks on Lake Erie Beaches." *Cleveland Plain Dealer*, September 17, 2019. https://www.cleveland.com/news/2019/09/the-mystery-of-bricks-on-lake-erie-beaches.html.

———. "Tashmoo v. City of Erie in the Grandest Steamboat Race in the History of American Navigation." *Cleveland Plain Dealer*. https://www.cleveland.com/news/g66l-2019/03/f927f21cea7980/tashmoo-v-city-of-erie-in-the-grandest-steamboat-race-in-the-history-of-american-navigation.html.

Kelleys Island. "Frequently Asked Questions." https://kelleysisland.com/frequently-asked-questions.

Kelleys Island Chamber of Commerce. "Kelley's Island History." https://www.kelleysislandchamber.com/island-history.

Kellman, Rich. "The Angola Horror of 1867: Train Crash Led to Rail Safety." WBFO, January 4, 2011. https://www.wbfo.org/2011-01-04/the-angola-horror-of-1867-train-crash-led-to-rail-safety.

Keppel, Angela. "Buffalo's Canal District, Part 2: Dante Place—Buffalo's Little Italy." Buffalo Streets, April 4, 2014. https://buffalostreets.com/2014/04/04/canalpart2.

———. "Canal District, Part 3: Marine Drive—Public Housing and Canalside." Buffalo Streets, April 17, 2014. https://buffalostreets.com/2014/04/17/marinedrive.

———. "Canal Street, Buffalo. 'The Wickedest Street in the World.'" Buffalo Streets, March 31, 2014. https://buffalostreets.com/2014/03/31/canalpart1.

Kohl, Cris. "Guest Column: A Tale of Rum Runner Shipwrecked a Century Ago." *Windsor Star*, January 14, 2023. https://windsorstar.com/opinion/letters/guest-column-tale-of-rum-runner-ship-wrecked-a-century-ago.

Krejci, William G. *Lost Put-in-Bay*. Charleston, SC: The History Press, 2022.

Lake Erie Living. "The Wineries of Lake Erie." https://lakeerieliving.com/articles/septemberoctober-2011/the-wine-regions-of-lake-erie.

Lake George. "History of the Comet at the Great Escape." https://www.lakegeorge.com/history/comet-roller-coaster.

LaMotte, Richard. *The Lure of Sea Glass: Our Connection to Nature's Gems*. Bishopville, MD: Sea Glass Publishing, 2015.

———. *Pure Sea Glass*. Chestertown, MD: Sea Glass Publishing, 2004.

Leary, Thomas, and Elizabeth Sholes, with the Buffalo and Erie County Historical Society. *Buffalo's Pan-American Exposition*. Charleston, SC: Arcadia Publishing, 1998.

Leskovec, R.A. St. Joseph High School Radio Club. http://www.sjhrc.org.

Lighthouse Friends. "Cleveland Harbor Main Entrance, OH." https://www.lighthousefriends.com/light.asp?ID=282.

———. "Vermilion Lighthouse." https://www.lighthousefriends.com/light.asp?ID=280.

Marble Collector's Society of America. "Earthenware Marbles." https://www.marblecollecting.com/marble-reference/online-marble-id-guide/earthenware.

Mauter, Ron. "Ironville Photo Scrapbook." Compiled 1996–2011. Toledo Lucas County Public Library. https://tlcpleasttoledo.omeka.net/exhibits/show/east-toledo/ironville, https://www.ohiomemory.org/digital/collection/p16007coll33/id/96412.

Middle Bass Island. "Lake Erie Islanders: Rudolph Siefield of North Bass Island." http://www.middlebass2.org/island_history_people_SiefieldNB.shtml.

Morona, Joey. "25 Restaurants from Cleveland's Past We Really Miss." *Cleveland Plain Dealer*, August 7, 2018. https://www.cleveland.com/life-and-culture/erry-2018/08/99a2e694e23166/25-restaurants-from-clevelands.html.

Museum of Women Pilots. "Women Pilots: Blanche Wilcox Noyes." https://www.museumofwomenpilots.org/women-pilots-blanche-wilcox-noyes-40.htm.

National Aviation Heritage Area. "1929 National Women's Air Derby." https://visitnaha.com/1929-national-womens-air-derby.

National Museum of the Great Lakes. "Ironville." https://nmgl.org/ironville.

Nelson, S.B. *Nelson's Biographical Dictionary and Historical Reference Book of Erie County*. Erie, PA: S.B. Nelson, 1896.

News5Cleveland. "Have You Ever Wondered Why These Steps and Wall Are at the Corner of Main Avenue and West 9th?" https://www.news5cleveland.com/

news/local-news/cleveland-metro/have-you-ever-wondered-why-these-steps-and-wall-are-at-the-corner-of-main-avenue-and-west-9th.

New World Encyclopedia. "Lake Erie." https://www.newworldencyclopedia.org/entry/Lake_Erie.

New York Times. "Three Go Down with Ship: Schooner Sunk in Collision with Steamer on Lake Erie." September 28. 1909.

Niagara This Week. "Did You Know…Erie Beach Had the World's Largest Swimming Pool." https://www.niagarathisweek.com/opinion-story/3259314-did-you-know-erie-beach-park-had-the-world-s-largest-swimming-pool.

O'Connell, Wil, and Pat O'Connell. *Ohio Lighthouses*. Images of America series. Charleston, SC: Arcadia Publishing, 2011.

Ohio Department of Natural Resources. "Lake Erie Geology." https://ohiodnr.gov/discover-and-learn/safety-conservation/about-ODNR/geologic-survey/lake-erie-geology.

Ohio Memory Collection. "Kelley Island Lime and Transport Company Insurance Report." https://ohiomemory.org/digital/collection/p267401coll36/id/11909.

Olin, Saul C. *The Story of Fairport, Ohio: Official Souvenir Edition. Commemorating Fairport's Sesquicentennial Celebration 1796—1946.* Fairport, OH: Neal Print Company, 1946.

Ollila, Saul. *Hometown Sketches, 1796–1936.* N.p., n.d.

1,000 Towns of Canada. "Old Erie Beach Amusement Park." https://www.1000towns.ca/old-erie-beach-amusement-park.

Painesville Telegraph-Republican. "'Frenchy': Thompson Unique Character in County Had Interesting History; Was Squatter For Years." 1914.

Pearson, George W. "Ironville Owes Its Name to Furnace Built in 1863." *Toledo Blade*, August 1938.

Pelletter, Louis F. "The Tragic End of the Steamship George Washington." Facebook, February 18, 2022. https://www.facebook.com/2071493269600058/posts/the-tragic-end-of-the-steamship-george-washingtonby-louis-f-pellettersilver-cree/4939289689487054.

Pennsylvania Department of Conservation and Natural Resources. "History of Presque Isle State Park." https://www.dcnr.pa.gov/StateParks/FindAPark/PresqueIsleStatePark/Pages/History.aspx#:~:text=As%20legend%20has%20it%2C%20many,Bay%20by%20the%20surviving%20sailors.

Public Broadcasting Service. *The Original North Pole.* https://www.pbs.org/video/wviz-pbs-ideastream-specials-original-north-pole.

Put-in-Bay Online. "Hotel Victory: Put-in-Bay's 'Grandest' Memory." https://putinbayonline.com/hotel-victory-put-in-bays-grandest-memory.

Rainey, Lee. "Lake Erie Limestone Carriers: The Shays of Kelleys Island." *Railroad Model Craftsman* (December 1986). https://kelleysislandhistory.blogspot.com/2020/12/a-history-of-kelleys-island-lime.html.

Roy, Chris. "Captain Frank's Lobster House: A Particularly Fishy Experience." Cleveland Historical. https://clevelandhistorical.org/items/show/901.

———. "S.S. *Aquarama*." Cleveland Historical. https://clevelandhistorical. org/items/show/766?fbclid=IwAR2VOIGfJEvBlx_NUT0rO5QkaBQx4-F9GUS55NUfl3-2bPq9EciOj3Qcbbc.

Rutherford B. Hayes Presidential Library and Museum. "Eveready Company." https://www.rbhayes.org/collection-items/local-history-collections/eveready-co.

Ryall, Lydia Jane. *Sketches and Stories of the Lake Erie Islands*. Norwalk, OH: American Publishers Company, circa 1913.

SamCooks. "America's Island Appellation." http://www.samcooks.com/americas-island-appellation.

Sandusky History. "The Capsizing of the Sandsucker Kelley Island." Blog, May 3, 2019. http://sanduskyhistory.blogspot.com/search/label/Shipwrecks.

———. "Enterprise Glassworks." Blog, April 4, 2019. https://sanduskyhistory. blogspot.com/2019/04/enterprise-glass-works.html?m=1&fbclid=IwAR3mHE OPrvD844Ayzi_Yi0rnUpSUnzgvxGwbunnRtudzNYksLWDOJq2wpoA.

Sandusky Register. "Deckhand Rescues 3 Crew Men." May 3, 1925.

———. "Trapped in Sandsucker Kelley Island as Vessel Capsizes Off Pt. Pelee." May 3, 1925.

Sangiacomo, Michael. "Titanic 100th Anniversary: Son, Grandson Marvel at How Anna Turja Survived Ship's Sinking." *Cleveland Plain Dealer*, April 8, 2012. https:// www.cleveland.com/metro/2012/04/titanic_100th_anniversary_son.html.

Schwartz, Brad. *The 1936–1937 Great Lakes Exposition*. Charleston, SC: Arcadia Publishing, 2016.

Sea Glass Journal. "The Sea Glass Shard of the Month, May 2014: Vitrite Sea Glass from Lake Erie." https://www.seaglassjournal.com/seaglassofthemonth/14-05-vitrite.htm.

Shea, John Charles. *Songs and Romances of Buffalo*. Buffalo, NY: C.W. Moulton, 1900.

Sherry, Jeff. "Erie County's Early Native Americans." Erie History, September 9, 2022. https://www.eriehistory.org/blog/erie-countys-early-native-americans.

———. "John S. Hicks: Erie Confectioner and Ice Cream Manufacturer." Erie History, February 24, 2023. https://www.eriehistory.org/blog/john-s-hicks-erie-confectioner-and-ice-cream-manufacturer-2.

———. "'We Have Met the Enemy…' Perry's Victory on Lake Erie, September 10, 1813." Erie History, September 10, 2021. https://www.eriehistory.org/blog/we-have-met-the-enemy-perrys-victory-on-lake-erie-september-10-1813.

Silver Creek Historical Center. "Burning of the Steamship Erie." March 8, 2019. https://www.facebook.com/profile/100064938270807/search/?q=erie%20 steamship.

———. https://www.facebook.com/profile/100064938270807/search/?q=erie.

Stahl's Auto. "1907 Pope-Toledo Type XV Touring." https://www.stahlsauto. com/automobiles/1907-pope-toledo-type-xv-touring.

Stimac, Mike. *The Visionary Life & World Adventures of Mike Stimac*. N.p.: self-published, 2012.

Stone, Joel. *Floating Palaces of the Great Lakes: A History of Passenger Steamships on the Inland Seas*. Ann Arbor: University of Michigan Press, 2015.

Sykes, Tim. "Remembering Crystal Beach Park." Wayback Times. https://www.waybacktimes.com/history/remembering-crystal-beach-park.

Tarrant, Rich. "The Crystal Beach in Vermilion Ohio: The Park of a Thousand." Vermilion Chamber of Commerce. http://www.vermilionohio.org/crystalbeach.html.

———. "Should Auld Acquaintance Be Forgot: McGarvey's Landing." Vermilion Chamber of Commerce. http://www.vermilionohio.org/vermviews/vermviews-302.htm.

Terry, Shelley. "Ashtabula's Titanic Survivor." *Star Beacon*, April 13, 2012. https://www.starbeacon.com/news/local_news/ashtabula-s-titanic-survivor/article_211147d6-5b37-5000-9f94-3926d9f41c19.html.

Thompson, Captain Merwin Stone. *An Ancient Mariner Recollects*. Oxford, OH: Typoprint, Inc., 1966.

Toledo's Attic. "The Birth of Toledo's Auto Industry." https://toledosattic.org/97-exhibit-themes/commercial-indistrial-history/176-earlyauto-essay?start=2.

Topp, Walter. "'Don't Give Up the Ship': Inside Oliver Hazard Perry's Triumph at the Battle of Lake Erie." Military History Now, May 7, 2019. https://militaryhistorynow.com/2019/05/07/dont-give-up-the-ship-inside-oliver-hazard-perrys-triumph-at-the-battle-of-lake-erie.

Vermilion Historical Society. "The History of Crystal Beach Park." April 8, 2019. https://www.vermilionhistory.org/articles/params/post/1762852/the-history-of-crystal-beach-park.

Vintage Menu Art. "McGarvey's Restaurant." https://vintagemenuart.com/products/mcgarveys-vermilion-oh-1930s.

Washington Post. "Blanche Noyes Was Pioneer in US Aviation." October 1981. https://www.washingtonpost.com/archive/local/1981/10/19/blanche-noyes-was-pioneer-in-us-aviation/08391b90-e60c-4a36-8156-a704af9971bf.

Westfield New York. "History." https://westfieldny.com/living-here/history.

Wolff, Carlo. *Cleveland Rock & Roll Memories*. Cleveland, OH: Gray & Company, Publishers, 2006.

ABOUT THE AUTHOR

Jennifer Boresz Engelking is the author of *Lost Lake County, Ohio* and *Hidden History of Lake County, Ohio* (published by The History Press). She is a Cleveland State University graduate and award-winning and regional Emmy–nominated writer who has worked in print and broadcast journalism. Jennifer has been published in magazines and newspapers, including *Echoes Magazine*, the *News-Herald* and *Lake Erie Living*; was a reporter for several years at CBS stations in Toledo, Ohio, and Erie, Pennsylvania; and has written and co-produced historical documentaries that have aired on PBS. She even once played a reporter in the Tony Scott–directed film *Unstoppable*. Jennifer was born, raised and still resides in Lake County, Ohio, near the shores of Lake Erie, and enjoys exploring nearby beaches, islands and parks with her husband and three children. Her website is www.jenniferboresz.com.